NASTY PEOPLE

Revised Edition

How to STOP BEING HURT by them without stooping to THEIR level

Jay Carter, Psy.D.

McGraw Hill

New York Chicago San Francisco Lisbon London Madrid Mexico City
Milan New Delhi San Juan Seoul Singapore Sydney Toronto

The McGraw·Hill Companies

Library of Congress Cataloging-in-Publication Data

Carter, Jay.
      Nasty people / Jay Carter. — rev. ed.
          p.   cm.
      Includes bibliographical references (p.).
      ISBN 0-07-141022-8
      1. Criticism, Personal.   I. Title.

  BF637.C74C37   2003
  158.2—dc21   2002041527

Some of the material herein was originally published in a slightly different form in the author's book *Self-Analysis*, © 1979 by James J. Carter.

19 20 21 22 23 24 25 26   QFR/QFR   1 5

ISBN 978-0-07-141022-9
MHID   0-07-141022-8

Interior illustrations by Daniel J. Hochstatter
Interior design by Nick Panos

McGraw-Hill books are available at special quantity discounts to use as premiums and sales promotions or for use in corporate training programs. To contact a representative, please visit the Contact Us pages at www.mhprofessional.com.

*Dedicated to our
great-great-grandchildren*

Contents

Acknowledgments

Many thanks to the following people for their help with the book: Linda Aglow, Dr. Astrid Jimenez Alvarado, Sandra DiSantis, Stanley Dudkin, Lotis Gudez, Dr. Monica P. Hottenstein, Dr. Sanford Mintz, Art Parker, Dr. Orest M. Pawluk, Stacy Prince, Jan Radabaugh, Sheila Sen-Carter, Dr. Margaret Verhulst, Nickie Williams, Anne Marie Zagnojny, Dr. Loretta Halpine-Martin, Dr. David O'Connell, and all my students. A special thanks to my literary agent, Sherrill Chidiac; to Dave Leiter for his encouragement; and to Barbara Karesh-Stender.

From a Student

I first met Jay Carter through his Communications Workshop at a local adult evening school. I signed up for the course to help in my never-ending search for better-spoken expression. The course helped *my* speaking, but it was really about something else. It was about people, and how they think and act. In other words, it was a course in practical psychology.

As part of this course, Jay taught us about invalidation. Invalidation is what I used to call "putting other people down to bring yourself up." But even though I had discovered the phenomenon of invalidation on my own, I didn't know where it came from, why it existed, how it really worked, or what to call it. Most important, I had no idea how deadly it could be to life, liberty, and the pursuit of happiness.

What I learned in Jay Carter's class about invalidation has changed my life. Now, at the very least, when invalidation is used in my presence, I know it instantly—whether it comes from someone else or from me (blush). I do my best to educate those involved about the "mechanics" of invalidation. To do this, I passed out copies of Jay's paper on invalidation.

After a while, though, copying and distributing those pages got to be a lot of work. Besides, at that rate, only about one person in ten million will ever learn what invalidation is all about. It's too important to keep it a secret.

So I've nagged, bullied, and generally pestered Jay into writing this little book on invalidation. I think you'll be glad I did.

L. David Leiter

From the Author

Every book has a story behind it, and I thought you might like to know the story behind this one. My motivation to gather the information presented here came from my own situation. I felt unhappy and didn't know why. I felt as if I were stuck in some sort of trap that I couldn't identify.

While I was pursuing my graduate degree in psychology, I kept a journal in which I wrote about my personal experiences, meetings with clients and professionals, and course readings. After a while, I began to notice that some of the dysfunctional features I was reading about were evident in people I knew. Then one day, while I was away on business and out of my daily environment, it hit me. I realized, objectively, that I was being invalidated—constantly.

When I first acknowledged how much I had been invalidated, I was enraged. It took me months to work off this anger. I wrote a lot of negative things about invalidators. I ran hard and fast. I purchased a punching bag. I chopped wood with a vengeance. I screamed obscenities when I was alone in my car. I passed my writings around to people so they could help me agree what terrible, no-good people invalidators are. I hated invalidators. I was out to get them.

Then one day, I shared my writings with a good friend at work. I had always admired this man. I called my collection of writings "The Invalidator."

He came back to me in tears saying, "I'm an invalidator. I've been making my mother miserable for years."

I was taken aback! I didn't want to believe him. He asked me, "How can I stop?" I stumbled over myself; I had nothing to tell him. My whole agenda had been to attack invalidators, not to help them. Driving home that evening, I realized that I had become an invalidator. I thought of my friend and his plight, and I cried. How could I have been so unaware? I had only written half a book! What about the invalidators themselves? How could they be helped?

I began looking for answers. I was serious and less enraged. I threw myself in front of invalidators just to see what happened. (You know what happens when you lie on railroad tracks? A train passes over your body.) I studied parents of invalidators. I studied criminals. I studied double-bind theory and every book I could get my hands on.

Finally I saw the whole cycle. I understood the importance of "the truth, the whole truth, and nothing but the truth."

Once I understood everything, my self-esteem returned. I was able to handle people better. Instead of spitting and hissing at invalidation, I could handle it with humor or by being confrontational and direct. I was no longer affected by invalidation. Instead of feeling outraged, I just felt a little nudge. Instead of attacking invalidation like Rambo, I would merely put it out with the rest of the garbage.

Once I discovered the secret to my own unhappiness, I began sharing my new understanding with others, and I saw it make a real difference in their lives. I witnessed miracles when I taught adult school classes.

At first, I presented students with my solutions to invalidating behavior. As time went on, however, I found it worked much better if I just presented the problem and allowed people to come up with their own solutions. We each make our own set of keys to life. We make each notch in each key from our experiences and the advice of others, sometimes through sheer luck or the grace of God. These keys unlock the secrets of life for us. Every once in a while, someone stumbles on a master key—a key that helps others create their keys more easily. I am sure I am not the only one who discovered the master key outlined in this book. In some ways, anyone could have written it.

By the time people started bugging me to write a book, I'd begun to realize that I had to do it. I needed to reach as many people as possible with my exciting discoveries.

Most teachers tell you that teachers learn as much from their students as students do from their teachers. I know that when I'm teaching, I always "find" an answer to a question, even if I didn't know that answer to that question before. I often find myself saying, "So that's it!" after responding to a new question. I had the same experience when writing *Nasty People*. In the midst of writing drudgery . . . bam! The cause of poor self-esteem was sitting there staring at me—the major cause, perhaps the only cause. It seems I had found another key, the key to self-esteem.

What you are paying for in this book is perspective. I have worked very hard, with the assistance of many people, to present this perspective to you in a simple and concise way. I don't care for books that force me to run through three hundred pages just for an idea that could have been presented in thirty. I've tried to spare you that. I've made an additional effort to cut out technical terms and keep the book small enough so you don't lose the big picture for the details.

How do I know these ideas are on target? Because people have told me they are. I have presented this perspective to thousands of people in universities and industry.

The concepts in this book may not make you happy. But they may make things clear enough so that you can stop being unhappy. I'll leave it up to you to do what you need to do to make yourself happy. For a start, let's get the monkey (whoever he, she, or it is) off your back.

I mentioned earlier that I had to write this book. For what good would my "master key" do my great-great-grandchild if invalidation is still running rampant? Did you know that the average person has 512 great-great-great-great-great-grandchildren? Here's to them!

It has been almost fourteen years since the first edition of this book was published, and it still sells well. It has been referenced by bestsellers, and it is probably the most perfect thing I have ever done. When I was asked to update it, I was hesitant. But I have learned more about invalidation over the last decade or two, and these things may be useful to others. I have received thousands of letters from people, and I have read every single one. Most of these letters were ones of relief. The book helped them put their situation in perspective. These letters have been invaluable. I am glad to see my book provided relief to people who were suffering so much, and I thank everyone for their letters.

Thanks to your letters, I am ready to take *Nasty People* to the next level.

I didn't want to change the format of this book, so the new material is interspersed throughout it. The new material deals with the following:

- **The captain of your soul.** Besides God, the captain of your soul should be you. Not only should it be you, it *is* you. Find out how to get your captain's hat back from the bully who took it.
- **Self-doubt.** Where does self-doubt come from?
- **Confidence.** Where does confidence come from?
- **The attribution of lesser motives.** Did you ever have someone indicate (or make it up) that your motives for doing a certain thing were lower motives or different motives than they really were? It makes you feel as if this person doesn't really know you, even if he or she is a loved one who should know you better. You end up feeling awful and desperate to have that person understand you.
- **Taking it personally.** Not taking things personally is one of the secrets of anger management and a secret to coping with invalidation.

- **Awareness of the bigger picture.** Maintaining awareness of the bigger picture is another secret of anger management and coping with invalidation.
- **Bullies.** Remember the school bully? Well he or she grew up and may now be your boss, or spouse, or professor, or roommate. He or she will be the same old bully but with more subtlety and polish. This understanding will help your kids and make you wish you had it when you were a kid.
- **Becoming bigger than your situation.** The magic of thinking big can help you in your struggle.
- **Blame.** Blame takes your power away. It's hard to take the reins to your own life when you are pointing at someone else (even if it *is* his or her fault).
- **Evil (violation of the human spirit).** One woman wrote about her invalidator, "It seemed that he was trying to kill my very soul." Not all people who do terrible things are sick. Some people are willfully evil.

It has been my experience that some will react strongly to this book. My heart goes out to them. Those who have been victims of invalidation may become enraged. Those who recognize themselves as invalidators may become sad or remorseful. Trust your feelings. If you feel sad, cry. If you feel angry, get mad. Don't hold it in. Let it out—appropriately, of course. Remember these are your feelings. Don't dump responsibility for your own feelings on anyone else. Blaming other people will not help, even if they are to blame. As you will see, blaming gives your power away.

Overview

This book is about that sector of the population that contributes to a specific phenomenon called *invalidation*. Invalidation could very well be the major cause of poor self-esteem, mental anguish, and overall unhappiness. With this in mind, you can see that this book may contain some of the most important information you've ever read and may significantly change your life.

Invalidation is propagated in our society by all of us. Only 1 percent of us intentionally spreads this misery to manipulate and control others. Twenty percent of us do it semiconsciously as a defense mechanism. The rest of us do it only occasionally, usually unconsciously and unintentionally. Invalidation can be found to greater and lesser degrees in various societies. Happier individuals develop in societies in which invalidation is at a minimum. Take, for example, the Philippines, a poor country without many natural resources other than its people. Their work ethic includes building up others rather than competitively tearing them down. In my experience there, I found very little invalidation. Despite their poverty, I found most people there to be warmhearted and generous with what little they had. Filipinos lose respect for those who tear others down.

Invalidation is a general term that I use in this book to describe one person injuring or trying to injure another. An invalidation can range anywhere from a shot in the back to a "tsk, tsk." A rolling of the eyeballs can be an invalidation, and so can a punch in the nose. It is usually the sneaky mental invalidations that cause the most damage. A punch in the nose is obvious, and it heals. However, an attack on self-esteem—at the right moment and in the right way—can last a lifetime. Destroying a person's capability to be happy for a whole lifetime is probably worse than any physical damage one person can do to another. The major reason invalidation occurs so often is that it works (in the short run). The sneaky invalidation works because a punch in the nose is obvious and can be returned to the insulting party, but the mental attack may go unnoticed and unpunished while it injures and manipulates its victim.

What if the process of invalidation were exposed?

Long ago, germs were unseen and unknown, yet they wreaked havoc. When Pasteur detected all these little bugs running around the body, people got upset. They put Pasteur away. They called him a heretic. Nobody wanted to think of little bugs that you couldn't see crawling all over you and inside you. Today, thanks to Pasteur and others, germs are known about and combated.

By the same token, being in denial about invalidators will not solve anything. Putting them away won't help, either.

Curing underhanded invalidation might not be easy, but it is much easier than dealing with germs; we won't have to invent antitoxins or penicillin. The big part of the cure for invalidation is achieved when we simply spot it. Remaining undetected and unchallenged is what gives invalidation its power.

Nevertheless, the people who get invalidated allow themselves to be invalidated, and they are just as responsible as the people doing it are. It is every person's duty to learn to recognize and divert or defuse the devaluating attack.

If invalidation didn't work, nobody would do it.

Psychology books contain theories. The only thing that separates useful theories from useless theories is practical applicability. Pasteur's theory about germs would still be in some book or other and Pasteur would be an obscure historical figure if his ideas had not been used to revolutionize medical practice. The best, most interesting perspective is worthless if nothing changes when you use it. The perspective in this book has worked for hundreds of thousands of people. I hope it works for you.

THE INVALIDATOR

The small Hitlers are around us every day.
—ROBERT PAYNE

It's hard to recognize an invalidator, because a truly good one can bypass the scrutiny of your logical mind, and his victim will find himself feeling bad without knowing why. The invalidator is underhanded, and the person being invalidated is often unsuspecting except for knowing that he feels bad. The invalidator actually feels inferior to some other person, so he tries to make that other person feel small. Thus, the invalidator can control the victim. Have you met anyone like this? Whether you are completely aware of it or not, you probably have. You probably know one or several invalidators.

The invalidator uses various suppressive mechanisms to chop away at your self-esteem. He pretends to acknowledge something you are proud of and then later makes some negative insinuation about it. He feels out what you think your shortcomings are and then exploits them at calculated times when he knows you are vulnerable. The invalidator may persist in invalidating you until you succumb. He has to control you because he perceives you as being superior to him. He takes accusations that have "some truth," and fires them at you "in all honesty," "just being your friend," "to help you."

The difference between an invalidator and a real friend is that a real friend will tell you one negative thing about yourself and then back off to give you space to consider it. An invalidator will lay many of your faults out for you and persist until you feel as big as the period at the end of this sentence. An invalidator will pick out the qualities about you that are most important to you and then tear them apart. An invalidator will listen to you share something that you don't like about yourself and then later use it against you. This is all done in such a subtle way that you are unaware of it.

If you do confront an invalidator on what she is doing, she will say something like, "Oh, come on now! I love you. I'm your friend. Where did you get these silly ideas?" And she may really like you. She may really want to be your friend . . . but only on her terms and only after she has you in her control. She will make you look silly for even thinking such things about her. She may make you feel guilty or cheap in front of your friends for accusing her of invalidating you. She may get angry at you for your accusations.

Whatever she can do to invalidate you further, she will. If she really thinks you are onto her, she may apologize and then not invalidate you again . . . until later when you are unsuspecting.

In short, the invalidator does whatever is necessary to control you. He is control-crazy, and anytime he perceives himself to be not in control, he will be scared.

Portrait of an Invalidator

One of the most famous invalidators was Adolf Hitler. He was quite typical of the controlling invalidator. He was a brilliant man. He created beautiful pictures. He was a writer. He saved the lives of his comrades when he was in the regular army. He loved his dogs. He had a love relationship with Eva Braun. He spoke beautiful words, for example:

> Since 1914 when, as a volunteer, I made my modest contribution in the World War which was forced upon the Reich, over thirty years have passed.
>
> In these three decades only love for my people and loyalty to my people have guided me in all my thoughts, actions, and life. They gave me the strength to make the most difficult decisions, such as no mortal has yet had to face. I have exhausted my time, my working energy, and my health in these three decades.
>
> It is untrue that I or anybody else in Germany wanted war in 1939.

Not only was he eloquent, but he lived up to his promises. He brought Germany out of a recession, making his words credible. People believed in him. It seemed he was never to blame. He was righteous.

He never killed anyone face to face but got his followers to do it. The sight of the Jews being slaughtered sickened him. He barely looked the one time he witnessed it. He really believed in what he was doing. Before he gained power, he tried to commit suicide, but one of his friends (a superior officer) saved him from it.

If you had met Hitler, you might have thought he was charming. You would probably not have guessed what devastation he was capable of. The following are excerpts from *The Life and Death of Adolf Hitler* by Robert Payne (italics are my own, for emphasis):

> Hitler was the arch-destroyer, determined to stamp out and destroy everything in the world *that did not serve his purposes*.
>
> Yet the man who spilled so much blood, and was so bloodless, never dared to look at the dead or the dying, never visited a military hospital, and *never showed any sympathy* for the maimed, the wounded, the blind. He drove millions of people insane and millions died in his concentration camps. He had no conception of the suffering he had brought to the world; and had he known, it would have made no difference. When he traveled through bombed towns, he drew the window

shades for fear that the sight of the destruction he had caused would weaken his resolution. In darkness, behind shuttered windows, remote from the world as in a grave he terrorized the world he *never understood and never wanted to understand.*

He especially liked one portrait of himself with his eyes raised to heaven in angelic innocence. He also admired a portrait of himself in shining armor.

The voice is seductive, and his *logic*, if his premises are accepted, *is unimpeachable.*

He believes in his own absolute authority over the people.

In the present age we are only too aware of his existence, for he still walks among us.

It is strange that we do not speak about Hitlers in the plural. . . . The small Hitlers are around us every day, tormenting us with their promises, rejoicing in our weaknesses, demanding our trust, our votes, and our lives, while remaining totally indifferent to everything except their thirst for power. *Power to order the lives of other men consoles them for their own insufficiencies,* their lack of humanity. They must have power or perish, and it is all one to them if they misuse their power or crush others in their efforts to seize power.

So you see, these invalidators can be particularly nasty characters if they get into positions of power. And they are always, in fact, striving for positions of power because they are "small Hitlers" with an obsessive need to control people and events.

The more clever invalidators don't use their powers until it's absolutely necessary. The invalidator can appear to be quite friendly for a very long time. Then it comes time for a promotion in management, and it's either you or him. He chews you up and spits you out in front of upper management before you know what hit you—all the while, of course, being your good buddy. He will even invent perfectly logical reasons why you wouldn't have wanted the job anyway—that is, unless he wants to destroy you completely. Then he will just make you look bad in front of everyone for a long time. He might do all this with information you told him about yourself in confidence, when he so endearingly listened to you.

You've probably met many people capable of being invalidators, but it probably caught you off guard and perhaps you didn't understand how it worked. The next section of this book will explain the methods used by invalidators. Read it thoroughly, but keep in mind that there are many methods of invalidation and many ways to handle an invalidator. And the minute you handle an invalidation is the minute it starts looking for another outlet.

There are no "cookbooks" for handling invalidation. That's why this book is so small. You need to know the essence or nature of invalidation so you can handle it your way. In this book, I'll give you a few examples of how it can be handled, but once you see invalidation, you must find how you deal with it best. You need to develop a strategy that fits your own personality, temperament, and ethics.

Methods of the Invalidator

The invalidator has many methods at his or her disposal, including uncertainty; projection; generalization; judgment; manipulation; sneak attack; double message; cutting communication; building you up, cutting you down; and the double bind. Let's examine each of these methods.

Uncertainty

One method of an invalidator is to keep you in a constant state of uncertainty. She rarely gives you an answer—just vagueness with no commitment. She makes you feel unsure of your environment for long periods of time, until your adaptive ability begins to fail. The invalidator may do this in any number of ways.

For example, the invalidator will suddenly become understanding, lovable, and very nice to you. Things will remain this way until you become trusting. Then with one swift blow, she makes you uncertain again by means of criticism, insinuations, or suppressed rage. You may ask, "What happened? We were doing so well."

The invalidator answers, "What do you mean 'what happened?' Is something wrong?"

"Well, yes. You are not the same," you say.

The reply is "What?!" (Fire eyes turn on.) "Really! You are driving me crazy! I can never be sure what you are going to come up with next." Then she repeats your comment sarcastically and mockingly. "What happened? We were doing so well!"

And there you are in a state of uncertainty, again caught up in the projections of your favorite invalidator. And you say to yourself, "Gee, I guess she really wasn't aware" or "Maybe it's me. . . . Maybe I'm reading into things too much. Maybe I'm going crazy."

And just about that time, your invalidator looks at you oh, so very lovingly and concerned and says, "Oh, honey, maybe you should see a doctor, you just aren't acting like yourself." She runs her fingers through your hair with the utmost look of concern and says, "I wouldn't want anything to happen to my baby." A slight tear forms in the corner of her eye. "Go see Dr. Schmidt tomorrow, honey, and tell him about the problems you've been having." Then she quickly turns, sits back down on the couch, and reads the paper.

And then there are the times you think, "Maybe she's changed. She just let me buy a new car and told me she loved me. She's been telling me how wonderful I am for a week/month." Things are great for a while. Then inevitably, after you trust her again, she begins all over again with the criticisms, the insinuations, the anger. She has you trapped in a sickening feeling of uncertainty.

In a classic black-and-white movie, David Niven plays a suppressive man who feigns love for his wife yet sets it up so that she ends up doubting her own sanity. This makes her more and more dependent on him and gives him more and more control. Sometimes it is hard to believe that a human being can actually do this sort of thing to another human being. There was a woman who poisoned three of her husbands with an undetectable poison that caused them to endure a long and painful death. She did it to get the insurance money and their belongings. It happens, and all those kind of people are not in jail.

Projection

Projection is a psychological maneuver that can be explained rather simply. It is a favorite tool of the invalidator; he simply takes his own feelings and puts the responsibility for them onto another person, as if these feelings originate with the other person. A projection is more of a proje*ctile*.

For example, a person who doesn't like you says, "I don't think you like me." This statement perhaps gets you questioning yourself. It thereby puts the attention on you, and you start looking at your own feelings instead of noticing the other person's feelings. This provides a good hiding place for the other person. The one doing the accusing is often calling you to task for things he himself is doing.

Isn't it ironic that the one who lashes out at others for his negative feelings or misdeeds is often guilty of the same failings in thought, word, or deed? When someone attacks you for something you didn't do, it says more about him than it does you.

For example, if I were a dedicated husband and my wife started accusing me of cheating on her, I would know almost for sure that she had done it in thought, word, or deed. You can tell an enormous amount about people by their projections. Listen closely.

Generalization

Watch out for generalizations. An invalidator will often use generalizations, which are simply exaggerations of small truths. The more truth there is in a generalization, the more it can be exaggerated.

For example, when you get home from work, your spouse might greet you with, "You are inconsiderate." (Translation: You forgot to bring home the milk.) "You are irresponsible." (You forgot to bring home the milk.) "You are stupid." (You forgot to bring home the milk.)

She attacks your self-esteem instead of the problem. The problem is there's no milk. The problem is not that you are inconsiderate, irresponsible, or stupid.

Even if you were stupid, what could you possibly do about it? How can you solve the problem of being stupid? (Supposedly if you went back to the store to get the milk, your IQ would increase by leaps and bounds!) A person who uses generalizations like this does so to be in control of another.

There could be a gender issue here. A woman may say, "You are so irresponsible!" in relation to specifically forgetting the milk. A man may take it as a hit to his self-esteem, taking it literally and generally when it was not meant that way or meant so strongly.

Judgment

Whether or not it was meant in a general sense, the preceding example still contains another of the invalidator's methods: judgment. The person who says "You are irresponsible" is passing judgment on you and further implies "Everyone would agree that you are irresponsible, obviously so."

And then, since you also might agree that forgetting the milk was irresponsible, you might assume that perhaps you are irresponsible. You begin to question and doubt yourself, especially if your inadequacies are pointed out frequently.

A person who is really responsible for his feelings would say, "I am angry that you didn't bring home the milk." But the invalidator acts as if everyone would agree with his or her judgment. In doing this, the invalidator attacks your self-esteem instead of the real problem.

This is a simple explanation, but perhaps you can think of times when a generalization or judgment really had you going. Especially if the judgment about you was made by someone you love or respect. You were upset by this judgment even if you don't think of yourself as stupid, or irresponsible, or whatever negative attribute the invalidator was attaching to you. After all, you don't want him thinking that of you, so you are motivated to make him understand, to please him, to get him to remove the unpleasant attributes he's attaching to you. All the while, of course, he is in control of the situation.

Manipulation

Manipulation is bad control. There is such a thing as good control. Good control is ethical and includes a fair exchange, "please," and "thank you." The invalidator wants to control . . . period. If good control fails, she uses bad control. If the usual methods fail, she uses devious, covert, or overt methods, because she is compelled to win or to be in control. You may often be pressured to let her have things her way. She will use sneaky methods of manipulation or outright methods of domination. An invalidator by definition is a manipulator.

Here's an example. Let's say your boss wanted you to work overtime. You tell her you can't because you are coaching your son's baseball team. She makes comments about how there needs to be dedication in the department. You remind her that you put in an extra twenty hours last week. She hopes you enjoyed the extra pay for those hours, alluding that you didn't do it out of dedication; you just wanted the extra money. You actually did it to help her out, and it causes you anxiety to think that she is attributing lower motives to your efforts. You realize that she did not appreciate what you did and she doesn't understand you. She goes on to say that the overtime pay is nice, but this is the day she *really* needs you. You tell her you are sorry, but there are a bunch of kids waiting for you on the baseball field and you can't let them down. She says that people let each other down all the time and if you let a person down when they really need you, you may be letting yourself down someday.

She presses you to think about the bigger picture (job security, promotion, etc.) to get you to forget about your present commitment and do what she wants. If she is a "crusader" boss, she will always expect extra out of her employees, and no matter what they do for her, she will remember the one time they disappointed her when it's time for the next job review. Crusader bosses take everything personally. If they get you to stay and work it is because they are so persuasive. If your department does well, it is because they managed their people well. Don't expect much from them. They will just work you to death and take all the credit. They are so far gone that they actually *believe* that they did it on their own. "Yeah, go play baseball with your kid. You won't get that pay raise, but you know what? You weren't going to get it anyway."

Sneak Attack

"I don't want to upset you, but . . ." (He probably does want to upset you.) "I don't mean to interrupt . . ." (Right!) "I don't mean to rain on your parade." (Uh huh.) "Don't let this bother you, but . . ." (Bother, bother.) "I hope this doesn't insult you, but . . ." (Here comes an insult!) The voice of the invalidator who uses the sneak attack will be soft. His face will show concern. His words are sweet, but underneath are daggers. The tongue is a mighty weapon, a sharp sword.

Double Message

The invalidator who is employing the double message says to you, "How are you?" But he verbalizes the words to you in something of a guttural tone—the voice of disgust.

If you respond with "Screw you, Jack!" then Jack will very innocently relate to everyone that you must be in a bad mood because all he did was ask how you were and you told him off. Jack will never come right out and say it, but he insinuates that you are a real son of a bitch . . . all the while making excuses for you (such magnanimity!).

It is well known that double messages in childhood contribute to self-doubt, uncertainty, and anxiety. The mother who says, "I love you," and then goes rigid when her child hugs her is sending a very destructive double message.

You may receive many double messages like this from an invalidator. But they may not be so obvious. Usually, you end up feeling weird or bad without realizing why.

For example, your friendly neighborhood invalidator might find out that your grandmother died and proceed to tell you stories about inheritance feuds. "You know, it's a shame sometimes when brothers and sisters go through estate settling and never speak to each other again." Then the invalidator will give you the facts (actually generalizations) about others she knows who have had family splits over inherited money. She will do this especially if she has a hint that you don't get along so well with one of your siblings. She is pretending to send messages of concern and love, but in truth she is throwing psychological daggers. Always look for the intent. Is this person just inappropriate, or does she have a motive? You can usually tell by the way she lives her life. Is she always gossiping? A passive-aggressive person like this enjoys causing an effect without taking responsibility for it. This person does not like direct confrontation and may start problems by playing the "let's you and she fight" game.

Why? Because some people feel so small they just want to create an effect. We did it when we were kids. I remember when I was a kid, my brother and I would be in the back of my father's 1952 Pontiac cruising down the road. We were both bored, so I would just quickly reach over and smack him a little, making sure my father didn't see. He would smile and smack me back. It would seem that he had hit me back harder than I had hit him, so I would smack him back, harder. This would continue until my father said, "Cut it out!"

We'd stay quiet for a while but we were still bored, so he'd smack me without my father seeing. It's game time again. We would continue to do this down the road and my father would repeatedly tell us to stop, but we know he can't really get us in the backseat, so we'd start up over and over again. Now it's more exciting because my father is getting angrier and angrier. It is interesting to see how far we can push him. It is our job, as children, to test the limits and boundaries of life. We would try to suppress our giggles. This would continue until we got my father so mad that he started swearing. Oops! So we'd cool it for a while and then start up again. We eventually made him so angry that he was psychotic and his backhand swept the backseat area trying to connect with one of us. (This was when smacking your children was not considered child abuse.)

So maybe it is human nature to do these things. Some of us just never grow out of it. We remain passive-aggressive like some children, but we have a fully mature cognitive ability so we get better at our childish games. Our double message to Dad was to tell him "OK" when he asked us to stop and then keep it up.

I can tell you this: Once we were made to take responsibility for it, the game wasn't so much fun anymore. If my father happened to connect with one of us, it ceased to be exciting. Or if we got home and my father made us clean the chicken coop, it didn't seem worth it. His message to us was that we were going to be responsible for our actions.

Make the person responsible for her actions. You might say, "Gee. What you are telling me could get me paranoid and start a real family feud!"

See what her response is to that. Her response to that will tell you if she is just being inappropriate or if she thinks she is sitting in the back of a '52 Pontiac.

Cutting Communication

Another valuable verbal tool for an invalidator is cutting communication. She asks you a question about yourself, then cuts you off before you finish answering. Or she asks you a leading question like, "Do you still quarrel with your wife?" You can't answer this question without appearing wrong. She walks out in the middle of a conversation, creating a logjam of unspoken thoughts piled up in your mind.

Building You Up, Cutting You Down

Be careful whom you depend on for your self-esteem. If you depend on others, the invalidator will shower you with compliments until you are totally dependent on him, then he will take you apart piece by piece until you are in his control.

The whole idea is to get you introverted and introspective so that you don't notice what is going on outside yourself. Once you start looking anxiously and self-consciously at yourself, the invalidator will subtly draw your attention to your most negative qualities. This will make you feel weaker, more susceptible to control.

By doing this, the invalidator can pull you down to size. He may feel that he worries too much, while you usually appear calm and confident. If he can get you to come down to his level and start worrying more, then he feels superior. And oh, by the way, he will be the first to offer to help.

After a while, you worry only about what he thinks, what he will do, whether he will be angry at you or not. You stop looking at yourself after a while because you see so much wrong with you that you totally depend on him for your sense of worth.

And then when even he doesn't want you . . . ?

The Double Bind

One of the meanest, sneakiest tricks of invalidators is the double bind. Logic will not solve this problem. Only awareness will solve it. The invalidator puts you in a position where you are wrong if you do and wrong if you don't.

This can be best demonstrated by an ancient lesson. Let's suppose you are a student of an ancient Asian institution of learning.

You show up at the master's house for your daily lesson. The master invites you in, and both of you sit down for a cup of tea. Just as you are ready to pick up your cup of tea, the master pulls out a large stick from under the table and says, "This is your lesson for today. If you pick up the cup of tea, I will hit you with this stick. And if you don't pick up the cup of tea, I will hit you with this stick."

I have presented this problem to thousands of people in my classes. Ninety-five percent of them have been so caught up in the logic of the problem and the thinking of a solution that they could not solve it. A typical answer is "Well, I would drink the tea. As long as I'm going to get hit anyway, I may as well enjoy it." Other people say, "I would slap the master in the face and get one in before he hits me."

There are two answers that will solve the problem. One is a good answer because it solves the problem while still

maintaining a relationship with the master. The answer is to take the stick away.

The other answer is to walk away. This answer solves the problem but cuts off further interaction with the master.

The whole beginning to the solution is to get out of the introversion-causing logic set up by the invalidator so you can view the whole situation. The whole situation involves you, the master, the logic, the game . . . the situation (big picture, context, etc.).

For example, right now, you are reading the words on this page. Your logical mind is right now interpreting these words and making sense of them. You could very well be introverted into this reading. You may not be aware of the whole environment you are in—the colors and sounds around you. We assume sometimes that when we read, we must concentrate on the reading so much that we cut off our other perceptions and only think. This is not necessary. You can read these words and still be aware of what's going on around you—what your feelings are, your body position, who or what is around you, and so on.

There is a certain feeling that goes along with a double bind, a feeling of being trapped. This feeling should be your cue to start being aware of your environment. This feeling should automatically make you stop thinking, stop introverting. Remove yourself from the immediate situation, and take a look at what's happening. Once an invalidator has you introverted and thinking, you are under his or her control.

The solution: Do not introvert. Do not take it personally. Step back and take a look. Do not defend yourself. Try to notice what makes the invalidator want to put you on the spot.

Let's look at an example of a double-bind situation.

A woman attending my classes was very excited about the work we were doing, feeling that she was getting a lot out of it. Her behavior was changing. She was regaining her confidence and becoming more self-assured.

Her husband was threatened by this and felt rather out of control. He gave her this ultimatum.

"It's either that damn class or our marriage." Logically, of course, the choice is easy. No one is going to give up a marriage just for the sake of attending a class. How would it sound to say to everyone "I gave up my marriage to attend Jay Carter's class"?

If her husband had constantly been threatening her this way, it might not have had such force. But he saved up this extreme type of threat, only calling on it on special occasions when he needed a large portion of control.

The wife popped out of her introversion and took a look at the game. She saw the typical elements of control.

1. It was his game.
2. It had the threat of a disastrous effect on her.
3. The outcome was all up to her. She was totally responsible for her reaction to his threat.

So what was the stick here?

Here is the way she handled it with him. She said, "I am not going to choose" (that is, "I'm not going to play your game"). "I am going to attend class, and you can choose . . . our marriage or this class." So, the stick was the choice.

To defeat the double bind, she used a technique I call *mirroring*. She threw the invalidator's game right back into his lap. When you give him the responsibility for his actions, an invalidator will almost always back down. All those threats he throws around don't just roll off the victim's back—they bounce, right back to him. If his victims use this technique frequently enough, an invalidator will eventually stop using his little tricks. Let's face it. If every time you kicked a dog it bit you, you would think twice before you kicked.

You may be wondering what happened to the guy and his wife. Well, they are fine. The more respect for herself she gained, the more respect he had for her. He stopped

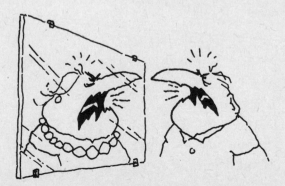

using the double bind on her when it stopped working. They went through a bad time for a while when she let out all of her pent-up anger on him. The tables reversed for a time with her as the invalidator and him as the victim. The invalidation eventually ran itself out, and the affinity bloomed again. They learned to get angry at one another in a more workable fashion.

It may not work out as well for everyone. Some people have built up resentment for so long that they cannot continue a relationship any longer. The relationship may have died, with only the double-bind control mechanisms still in place.

If there is any chance at all of reviving a relationship, I highly recommend it. People who are capable of being rotten are usually equally capable of being wonderful. I've seen people who use the mechanism of invalidation make 180-degree turns in attitude. I don't quite understand it because I myself change slowly. Nevertheless, once an invalidator learns to handle his anger and stops invalidating, he can make a sudden change and never do it again.

The understanding and willingness to do something about it are key factors. But beware of sudden changes that merely lead to further manipulation. If your beloved invalidator says he understands now what he's been doing and vows to reform but then is unwilling to discuss it again, don't trust him.

In a double bind, it is always the *situation* (context, big picture) that is the problem. Many times we can feel the bind, but we can't "see" it. So, then you should stop thinking (introverting) and feel it . . . and take a step back. After you stop and take that step back so you can see the bigger picture, you may be able to spot the double bind that shadows the whole situation. For example, a battered woman asked her husband, "Why did you hit me last night?"

He mulled it over, trying to think of a reason, and then said, "Because you burnt the spaghetti." She actually breathed a sigh of relief because she thought she could control it by not burning dinner. No! It is the *situation* that is the problem. She is married to a perpetrator of physical abuse.

As another example, take the woman who works for a misogynist (man who hates women) and doesn't get promoted. She asks her boss about it and he gives her some good-sounding reasons. He tells her that her work has mistakes in it. She has been late (five minutes a couple times in the last year). The bottom line is that even if she were the best worker in the world, she is not going to get the promotion, because the *situation* is that she works for a *misogynist*.

The Bigger Picture

One of the deliberate things an invalidator may do is fail to acknowledge the bigger picture. During your job appraisal, your invalidator boss may bring up mistakes you have made and compare you to Joe, who has made fewer mistakes. In doing so, the boss may fail to acknowledge that you have made twice as many mistakes as Joe has because you have done twice as much work as he has. Your boss then justifies giving you a low appraisal. When Joe comes in for his appraisal, your boss will compare Joe to you, telling Joe that he hasn't done as much work as you have. This is done consciously to rationalize giving you both a low appraisal. Why would a boss do that? Maybe because she doesn't want anyone having a higher appraisal than she has. Maybe because the boss is a megalomaniac. Maybe because your boss's boss told her to not be generous and your boss doesn't have the guts to stand up for you.

Now let's talk about unconscious invalidation. Most of us unconsciously invalidate others at times. We don't know we are doing it and we would change if we were aware of it. We do it to our kids, our spouses, our parents, and our friends. We do it because we are unaware of the bigger picture; we are not situationally aware. We do it out of ignorance and by taking things personally that are not personal. Let me explain why by discussing self-doubt in the next section. I bet you didn't think that section was about you, did you? Well, it is. I want to explain to you how people invalidate each other unconsciously. The only way to do that is to provide an example that you may not be conscious of. I do this lovingly. I do it so that you may have a little compassion for others who may not realize they are invalidating (as opposed to people who don't *care* if they are invalidating). Try not to feel guilty after you read the next section. On second thought, no, go ahead and feel guilty if you want to.

Self-Doubt

We collect so much self-doubt as children. In this section I am going to give you an example of how that happens. This is just one example, but one you perhaps didn't realize.

If a person had ADHD (attention deficit/hyperactivity disorder) when she was a child, she wouldn't be able to see the big picture of things. Kids with ADHD *can't* maintain a situational awareness of things. (Did I say *can't*? Oh good, because I meant to say *can't*.) So, when we put them in a classroom and they start talking to their neighbor, or can't sit still, we tell them they are rude and disrespectful. They end up believing they are really rude and disrespectful. We attribute lower, or suspect, motives to a kid who may not have any such motives, or who has no motives at all. One-third of these children "outgrow" ADHD. Actually, the prefrontal lobe of their brains kicks in about the age of twelve or so. After the prefrontal lobe is developed enough, they *can* see the bigger picture of things. They *can* see the context they are in. They *do* see the *situation* of things. They are no longer disrupting class, dinner, a funeral, etc. But now we end up with someone who believes he or she is rude and disrespectful—self-doubt, instilled by adults.

I made the mistake of taking my ten-year-old to a wake once. His prefrontal lobe hadn't developed yet, so I couldn't expect him to be situationally aware. People were crying, and then someone said something poignant and there was that silent period after. Out of the blue, my son started singing a little tune, inappropriately loud, "Do do do dum dum dee dee!" People stared at him. I was embarrassed and considered telling them that I didn't know who this child was. Yes, I know he came in with me, but he must be someone else's kid.

Adults soon forget what it is like to be a kid. Children don't have a situational awareness because their prefrontal lobes are not fully developed and they are unable to see the context of things, the bigger picture of things. That does not mean that we should invalidate children, just because our brains are more developed. Yet that is what we do, and we also do it to adults whom we do not understand. (Feel guilty yet?)

What happens to the two-thirds who have ADHD and do not outgrow it? Well, 32 percent do not graduate from high school. Gee, what a surprise! We drop these kids off at a cognitive school requiring heavy bouts of paying attention for hours and hours a day and we expect them to maintain a situational awareness, but we don't actually teach them how to do it and their temperaments are not inclined to do it. Of course, then we invalidate them when they can't do what we want and their behavior is inappropriate.

This is just one example of how self-doubt creeps into kids' lives.

Now, why do we do that? You are not going to like the word discussed in the following section.

Narcissism (Everything Is About Me)

I have never met a conscious invalidator who was not narcissistic. The rest of us don't mean to be narcissistic and we don't mean to invalidate. As we get older and wiser, we lose our narcissism but, with very few exceptions, there are still unconscious pockets of it in even the most enlightened human beings. We are all narcissistic to some degree. (Don't hate me for saying that yet!) When we are children, we think the moon is personally following us down the road at night. My six-year-old wanted to stay up all night. I said, "OK, you can, sometime." He pondered a little and then said, "Dad, if I stayed up all night long, would the sun still come up in the morning?" That was cute but narcissistic to think that the sun revolved around him.

If a teenage boy accidentally leaves his fly open, he gets so humiliated because *everyone* knows about it. A teenage girl might feel *sure* that everyone is looking at the zit on her face. Kids with big egos believe they are the greatest and the whole world revolves around them. Kids with poor self-esteem think that they are pieces of junk . . . that the whole world revolves around. As we get older and wiser we grow out of our narcissism, but I don't know anyone who has completely grown out of narcissism.

Narcissism is the same as *taking it personally*. Now here is my point. When the kid with ADHD is acting up in class, it is already a big enough burden to have to correct him when he interrupts the class. Why do we take on the additional burden of thinking that this child was being rude and disrespectful . . . to me, me, me? You see my point? The fact is he *wasn't* being rude and disrespectful. Isn't it already difficult enough? Do we need that additional burden of feeling disrespected? Taking that on is hurtful and we don't need to feel that way. Narcissism really doesn't help us cope—quite the opposite.

In my own case I remember having road rage because someone cut me off, and then *he* gave *me* the finger! I chased him down the road driving about two inches from his bumper and he became scared. And that fear made me happy! I didn't care that I was a psychologist. I didn't care that I was more than fifty years old. My prefrontal lobe was trying to get through to me as my whole life became about being two inches from his bumper. Finally my prefrontal lobe broke through with "Jay, you *teach* anger management!" That finally got to me and I slowed down. But later when I thought about it, it occurred to me that I took that incident personally (narcissism). When, actually, I could have been *anybody* and that guy was still going to cut him off and give him the finger. There wasn't anything personal about it whatsoever.

This is one of the great secrets of dealing with invalidation. Don't take things personally, because they usually are not personal. If you are married to a misogynist, all those lousy things he does to you are probably not personal. He would do those things to any woman he was married to. Is it upsetting? Sure. If I didn't take it personally when that man cut me off, would I still have been upset? Sure, I would, but I wouldn't have chased him down the road, risking my life and his.

So here you are reading this book about invalidation, and the author calls you a narcissist. Nice guy, huh? But I am only doing it because I love you. My intentions are good, and I think it will help you in the long run. If you are one of those people who says "See? It is *my* fault. I knew it! I am narcissistic," then go read *Codependent No More* and come back here and pick up where you left off. Some things are very difficult *not* to take personally. I know that. But it is either personal or it isn't, and it usually isn't.

Chemical Imbalances

Some people have chemical imbalances and they become nasty because of them. (If they don't have enough serotonin, for example, they could get depressed or irritable and feel hopeless.) Some nasty people have chemical imbalances and they become nastier because of them. A person who is bipolar may end up in jail for doing something crazy during a manic episode but it doesn't mean he has nurtured a criminal nature. (He may deserve a punishment of work release as long as he takes his medication.) A *criminal* who is also bipolar . . . that's different. Discerning between the two is important.

The most significant chemical imbalance related to nasty people comes from the *bipolar disorder*. People with bipolar disorder can be perfectly healthy psychologically, but due to a dopamine imbalance, become manic or depressed.

It is a hereditary and chemical problem. Their problem may be mild, moderate, or severe. If it is severe, they do not have much control. If they are manic, their thoughts race. They get very little sleep. They become angry-manic or euphoric-manic. They have mood swings, in which one minute they will be laughing and having a good time and the next minute they will be angry and in your face. During the mania, they get very little sleep, and so like anyone who gets very little sleep, they may become irritable and nasty. Their thoughts are probably racing six times faster than yours, and they have no filtering system (as if their brains are connected directly to their mouths). They may talk rapidly and say things that will rip your heart right out of your chest. They can be very invalidating. Their conscience is diminished during the mania, so they may do or say things that seem unconscionable. In their normal state of mind, they may be quite personable and conscientious. If you have friends or relatives who have this imbalance, you really need to *not* take what they say personally when they are manic.

Most of us *think* things we would never actually say, but mania can be a direct thought-to-mouth process. During the mania, the prefrontal lobe of the brain is diminished, so their judgment is poor, even though they may think brilliantly. They are not in tune to the bigger picture of things or the consequences of what they do. They may intellectually know what they are doing, but they are not engaged in the bigger picture. They feel good, and they may have what I call *the trilogy* operating: ego, arrogance, and entitlement.

I know you might think that people can always help what they say, but if you do think that, refer to the section above on narcissism. Sometimes they really can't help it. I am not trying to make excuses for them. I am merely trying to point out that it is not personal.

What do they need? Medication to balance them out. There are some very good medications out now. People with bipolar disorder may have to make a decision between maintaining their "natural high" or keeping their friendships (or marriages) intact. If you are the spouse of someone like this, you may have to have him or her decide whether to keep you and the meds or say goodbye to everything.

Personality Disorders

I really don't like to talk about personality disorders because I don't think there is such a thing as a personality disorder. I believe when a certain human with a certain temperament has a series of experiences, he or she ends up with what other people call a personality disorder. I have seen these so-called personality disorders go away with trauma work. I think they are trauma based, whether it is abuse trauma, pleasure trauma, family trauma, or a combination of trauma. When people experience a trauma, they tend to react strongly to things that resemble the stimulus that caused it. I was stung by bees when I was a child. When I see a bee, my body panics and adrenalin flows through my veins. Adrenalin stays in your veins for twelve to twenty minutes because it's a blood hormone. I react the

same way every time. I run from the bee. That's my drama
. . . running from the bee. I can't help it. It is a very dis-
associating experience.

I spoke to a mental health expert who does an all-day
seminar on personality disorders. He said the bottom line
is the *drama*. It's not about the *motive* or the *result*. It's
about the drama. That can be very confusing for you unless
you know that. You might be asking yourself, "What does
this person want?" The answer is that she wants the drama.
You may ask, "What does this person want to get from
this?" The answer, again, is the drama. She just wants to
"get into it" with you. And it's probably not planned by
her. You may remind her of someone or look like someone,
or it might be Christmas when she always gets this way.
Don't take it personally, but don't take it impersonally
either. For example, all I have to do to my wife is say something like, "And how do you feel about that?" She will say,
"What?! I am not one of your clients. Don't talk to me that
way." And she is right, because I am being impersonal and
objective.

I believe that personality disorders are triggered by
relationships.

Remember: Don't take it personally or impersonally.
Don't introvert. Be empathetic. It's probably not about you.

Invalidator: An Archetype

Do you remember a friend that you imitated? Do you act
like your mother sometimes? Your father? It could be said

that you entered into the archetype of your mother, father, or friend for that time you acted like them. An *archetype* was designated by Carl Jung as a complete personality type, one that recurs throughout human experience. Common archetypes are those of the warrior, the hunter, or the demon.

You probably have several personalities that you have developed yourself: your mom or dad role, your professional image, your "kid" personality. These are separate types that you develop and use every day. It's almost like having separate suits of clothing for different occasions in the closet of your mind. If you are a woman with children, you probably have your own "mom" personality. This might be made up of

- Your own ideas about what a mom should do and say, or how she should act
- Behaviors borrowed from your mom (including those things that you said you would never do to your kids but find yourself doing anyway)
- Behaviors borrowed from television moms, other people's moms, your grandmother, etc.

So what am I getting at here, anyway?

OK, let me paint a personality for you. Did you ever notice that most invalidators are not nasty people all the time? That's what makes them so difficult to understand sometimes. They are unpredictable! You never know what might set them off. (Sometimes you do know.)

All of a sudden, it's like a demon takes them over. This nice person becomes a ranting maniac, or else he becomes a very withdrawn, biting person. Or else he seems nice, but you suddenly feel bad around him without knowing why. There are various degrees of obviousness when invalidation occurs. And there is a psychological cycle that happens to each invalidator when invalidating behavior appears.

What follows are the three degrees of invalidating behavior from the most obvious to the most covert.

Most Obvious Personality

In his most obvious personality, the invalidator appears to have no conscience at all and sometimes seems crazed enough to be capable of anything. He seems about to lose control at any second. He exudes and reeks of anger, outrage, and righteousness. He threatens to do things that are the most liable to do you in. He may sometimes threaten to do outlandish things while smiling at you as if enjoying your plight, or he makes it appear that you deserve his disap-

proval, that you have surely done something to set him off. At other times he is overly loving and apologetic.

Sometimes too much liquor can turn on this demonic personality in a person.

Less Obvious Personality

In her less obvious personality, the invalidator points out your weaknesses. She reminds you of your past misdoings. She tries to get your agreement that things you do are wrong and is constantly proving how bad you are. She acts as if the good things you do aren't that great, or you finally did something good "for a change." She is righteous. When you point out to this person some wrongdoing of hers, she will bombard you with all of your wrongdoings, in an indignant manner. Her memory for recalling your mistakes is usually fantastic. Later, she may get upset, saying, "How could you say that about me? You hurt me." She proves to you what an ass you are. She is jealous of your possessions and envies your accomplishments. She belittles you in groups.

Least Obvious Personality

In his least obvious personality, the invalidator appears to be your good buddy. He always has some negative thing to tell you "in good faith." He loves to be "honest" and "truthful." He gossips about you behind your back and is secretly jealous of you. He tells you secrets about the negative things other people are thinking of you. He pays you compliments that are really double messages, insinuating that you are paranoid if you confront him on his double messages. It's possible he has a higher opinion of you than he has of himself.

At work, this person may get you to talk about yourself. He seems to be so interested in your life. You take it as friendship, but he never talks about himself. He is listening calculatedly. When a promotion is available and he feels he is competing with you, he may spill private things you have told him to your boss. He has no qualms about stepping on your shoulders to reach the next level.

As these descriptions of the three degrees of invalidating behavior indicate, nobody is an invalidator all the time. More often, a perfectly wonderful person turns from the one you love into a monster who hates you and can't think of enough ways to degrade you. Your loved one becomes temporarily like a demon. This demonic form is not all there is in this person; it is an archetype he or she enters at times. While someone is in it, this demonic personality is complete with its own thoughts, ideas, ethics, and behavior. A person may enter into this behavior consciously or may slip into it unconsciously when something in the environment triggers it.

The worst case is a Hitler who consciously goes into this personality at calculated times. In addition, a Hitler develops this archetype to perfection so that it works almost every time.

Most people slip into the invalidator archetype unconsciously, reacting to subtle and sometimes unnoticed cues in the environment. These poor people have been exposed to invalidators in the past—often a parent or sibling who just never could be pleased or approving. Unconsciously, without understanding the source of their trouble, they become invalidators at various unpredictable times. They are running on automatic pilot; they don't know what they are doing and they don't know what else to do. Sliding into this role is no great advantage, either to the victim or the invalidator. The invalidator can win a lot of battles with the behavior but in the long run loses the war. He or she may get to control others for a time, but after a while no one wants to be around an invalidator. Of course, some invalidators (like Hitler) are so clever and subtle that they always have others around them to control.

Identifying an Invalidator

Perhaps you have met someone who flattered you by being possessive and jealous. Then later you were puzzled when this person treated you condescendingly. This person would be interested in you especially when you had the attention of others but then become bored with you when you devoted most of your time to him. He might become enraged when you did something against his will or against his opinion. When you demonstrated you had a mind of your own, he became more enraged. Making love to this person would seem more like the satisfaction of his libido than a sincere expression of love. Everyone probably has these tendencies sometimes, but the invalidator has them to a great degree.

To deal with an invalidator, first you have to be able to detect one. Methods of invalidation can be so clever, so sneaky, and so suppressive that you might not be able to see them. If you know someone that you always feel bad with, it could be your insecurities or it could be an invalidator at work—probably both.

Simply stated, your insecurities come from past experiences that you never really noticed or understood or accepted that have been embedded in your subconscious and wait, ready to cause pain or defensiveness or introversion at odd moments when you least suspect they are at work. A clever invalidator finds your most sensitive spots and plays on them to gain control over you by making you feel vulnerable.

The important thing to look for is not the various traits of an invalidator but how you feel over a certain period of time when you are in the company of a possible invalidator. It is not necessary to see all the mechanisms an invalidator uses. Somewhere you will pick up the way things are going with this person.

I have learned over the years that there are some general traits that seem to be common among invalidators. These traits also exist in others, so they are not only in invalidators. There are three traits that I generally see together and call *the trilogy*:

- Ego
- Arrogance
- A sense of entitlement

What are these traits, really? An ego is needed where there is a lack of self-esteem. It looks like the person thinks she is hot stuff, but if you look deeper, her behavior is a smoke screen for not feeling good about herself. Arrogance fills in for a lack of confidence. If you don't have confidence, arrogance is a good smoke screen. And what is entitlement? I looked for the meaning of that for two years. I would see people come into prison feeling entitled. My wife was a nurse, and she would see it in the hospital. Someone would come in with no insurance, she would have her life saved by the hospital staff, and the next morning she would say, "Where's my cable TV?"

Entitlement hides a lack of accomplishment. Sometimes you will see it in school when a kid can't seem to pay attention, complete his homework, get good grades, etc. He can't *accomplish* anything so he thinks he needs to *take* it. I saw one kid save up his money for a mountain bike. He worked hard mowing lawns and finally bought this $300 mountain bike. His brother sold it for crack the next day. After that, I saw his sense of entitlement: "If I can't accomplish anything or earn anything, I just have to take it."

So here you have someone who seems to think he is great (ego), has confidence in himself (arrogance), and knows what he wants and walks around like he owns the place (entitlement). You might mistakenly think this person has it together. Wrong! If you see ego, arrogance, a sense of entitlement, and narcissism, be wary of invalidation. It may not come your way but there is a good chance it might, considering the aforementioned trilogy ingredients.

You should get enough data in this book to enable you to spot an invalidator. Follow what you feel you know. If you feel constant jabs of discomfort when you are with someone, take a look at what he or she is doing.

This book does not even begin to describe all the techniques of invalidation; there are a lot more tricks and traits to which a much longer book could be devoted. However, this book is not just about "things to watch for in others." My presentation of this material about the invalidator is not intended to make you paranoid. Don't read this information and become a recluse. Just notice that these forms of behavior exist in some people at some times, and be prepared to handle it when it does. These traits are described for you to know about so that you don't introvert on yourself.

I estimate that approximately 1 percent of the population is made up of bona fide conscious invalidators. Twenty percent of the population are "semiconscious" invalidators. If you are reading this book, the chances are excellent that you are not the 1 percent mentioned. Bona fide conscious invalidators would not want to attempt the self-improvement contained in this book. They don't need to. They already know why they do what they do. Confidence has a dark side. If you know what your intent is, you can get confidence from that. If your intent is to rip people off, you can get a calculating confidence from knowing this. You can feel superior because you have an edge. That's why they call them *confidence-men*.

While reading this book, you may notice yourself having intense feelings. Just keep plodding on through. You may need some time alone after reading parts of this book so you can reintegrate yourself. Allow your emotions to arise. Trust your feelings.

True invalidators are not easy to spot. But if you pay attention to your feelings and to people who are connected to invalidators, you will be able to recognize them. You will notice that people who are connected to invalidators are not in the best condition, while the invalidators seem just fine. The invalidator's family may seem to be all "mental cases," while he or she is the only sane one. It is actually just the opposite.

2

THE VICTIM

No one can make you feel inferior without your consent.
—Eleanor Roosevelt

Victims of invalidators can be compelled to remain victims. Most of us, for example, have a strong reaction to someone shouting at us. As children we were (perhaps) trained to respond to a raised voice by doing what was demanded of us. Now when a person raises his or her voice, some of us are moved to propitiate and do what is asked to avoid discomfort. Others of us will rebel and shout back, attempting to avoid the discomfort of feeling forced into something we object to. Both reactions are indicative of people who have been victims in the past. We learned how to dysfunctionally deal with such situations and find ourselves similarly reacting in similar situations.

How Victims Are Compelled to Remain Victims

You may choose to hang out with a bona fide member of the Invalidator Club. The Invalidator Club is a club that never has any meetings because the members don't enjoy each other's company. Seriously, if you choose to be connected to a true member of the nasty 1 percent, a bona fide conscious invalidator, because you think you can handle it, there are some things you should know. He has to control. It's survival for him—ego survival. If he sees himself as inferior to you, he will always feel compelled to reduce you so he can control you. The very first time you are sick or run down or in trouble, or in any way down, he will try to make sure you stay down. If you want to hang around playing that sort of game, it's your business. Your invalidator may be very charming and adventurous and probably very intelligent. If your invalidator turns you on, have fun while it lasts. Misery is around the next corner. You may think you'll never be in that vulnerable position of feeling "down." But by staying connected to a "one-percenter," you are creating it. So bon voyage. . . .

Allowing yourself to be under the constant stress of always having to react to an invalidator could lead to psychosomatic illness. I have known several people who were connected to invalidators by marriage or family. Some of these victims had ulcers, heart disease, cancer, Irritable Bowel Syndrome, and other disorders. Being under the daily stress of dealing with an invalidator does eat away at you even if you handle it very well (Drossman, 2000; Shorr, 2002). And usually with a true invalidator, you have to handle it, and handle it, and handle it . . . ad nauseam, ad infinitum.

If you do leave, the ranting, raving invalidator may suddenly get very soft and may even admit to invalidating. She will do anything to get you back under her wing. She will tell you how miserable she is without you.

Then when you feel sorry for her and decide to come back, she will secretly consider you a fool for being sympathetic. She will wait for a time, and then she will begin working to get you down again.

A true invalidator will say anything to keep you with him, because he has to have you—but not because he loves you. He has to have you because he has to control you, not because he loves you. He has to have you because you fulfill his desires for power, not because he wants you. He has to have you because you serve his purpose, not because he is interested in you. He is interested in you only so that he can find your weaknesses and play on them, to control you.

It doesn't matter whether an invalidator is conscious or unconscious of what she does. She is still responsible for it. It doesn't matter if someone shoots you consciously or unconsciously . . . you still die. In the case of invalidation, it's sometimes harder to deal with someone who is unconscious of doing it. When confronted with what she is doing, she may say, "Where did you get that silly idea? You are invalidating me by accusing me of invalidation!" After she says that, you will probably be ready to tear her apart. However, there are some things to consider. First of all, if she is unconsciously invalidating you, there's a good chance she has been connected to an invalidator (mother, father, boss, spouse). When she gets angry at you, it may come out as invalidation. Being an "unconscious invalidator" is very hard for any person to confront. No one wants to think of herself that way. Then again, it's not your problem that she doesn't recognize her problem. You must treat her as if she is conscious of it. In my opinion, the best you can do is (1) point it out, (2) stand your ground, or (3) disconnect if she is not willing to see it. She may come around only after she is faced with losing her relationship with you.

Creating a Victim

People are born willing to listen, but after many years of being put down, we may stop being willing to listen. People are also born willing to be wrong. But after an invalidator points out constantly what we do wrong, we may stop being willing to be wrong about anything.

Invalidators abuse a willingness to listen by making so many critical or cutting remarks that some victims close up and stop listening completely to escape the terrible feeling of always appearing to be wrong. This defense allows the victim to stop hearing the invalidator and stops some of the pain of invalidation. But the reaction to the invalidator may also cause her not to listen to anyone else, either. She may

try to appear totally righteous. The victim loses the willingness to listen and the willingness to be wrong. She becomes suspicious of other people's motives.

You may know someone who doesn't listen much and talks a lot. Was there an invalidator in her past?

Another person who has been injured by an invalidator may be very quiet and shy. He is afraid to open his mouth out of fear of being invalidated. He may seem to reject friendship with anyone, but that may spring from his fear. A shy person may be naturally quiet and reserved, or he may have been connected to an invalidator who stepped on his self-esteem whenever he spoke up for himself. There is a difference between choosing to be quiet and feeling stifled.

Still another product of an invalidator is someone who is very stubborn. She may call herself *strong-willed*. She has had it with invalidators, has decided to stand her ground no matter what, and will not change her mind under any circumstances. She is never wrong.

How can we correct our own behavior if we can't listen to others and if we can't afford to be wrong? The ruination of our God-given gift of communication is one of the most destructive things that one person can do to another. Equally devastating is the part we ourselves play when we allow someone else to force us to limit or distort our communication ability because of our fear of invalidation.

Right/Wrong Dysfunction

The normal functional process for most people who do something wrong is this:

1. We do something wrong.
2. We feel guilty.
3. We take responsibility for it.
4. We atone for it.

This is the most therapeutic, functional way to handle wrongdoings in our society and in our individual lives.

If we gyp someone out of ten dollars, we feel guilty. Then we tell them we gypped them and we give them the ten dollars back. Simple. Clean. Therapeutic. (You could throw in a couple of "Our Fathers" and "Hail Marys" if you wanted to do so.)

For some people, this is not within their perspective. Perhaps they have been wrong for so long that they can't be wrong one more time about anything. Their dysfunctional approach is this:

1. They do something wrong.
2. They can't feel guilt, so they instead *justify* what they did.
3. They can't take responsibility, so they *blame* the victim.
4. They can't atone for it, so they disrespect the victim and lower the victim in their eyes. After they do this, it is easier to repeat the first step.

I have presented this theory to many clergy in my seminars and have received positive feedback on it. The dysfunctional method seems to start a bad cycle that continues to repeat until the victim gets respect by confronting the perpetrator. The perpetrator may then feel punished and the bad cycle is temporarily stopped (until the next time).

In more detail, most people are familiar with what might happen when Joe hurts Fred: Fred then may be motivated to hurt Joe. It's very simple. Someone does something to hurt you, and then you might want to do something to hurt him back.

However, what most people are not aware of is the following sequence of events:

1. Joe hurts Fred (i.e., Joe invalidates Fred).
2. Fred is unaware that Joe hurt him, but nevertheless Fred feels bad.
3. Joe sees that Fred feels bad and also sees that Fred is not going to return the hurt.

4. Joe can't allow himself to be wrong (feel guilty). In order to be righteous about his actions, Joe begins to invent "reasonable" excuses about why he hurt Fred. He looks for justifications for having hurt Fred. Joe may say to himself, "Well, anyone who would let me walk all over him deserves to be hurt." Or he could say, "That's just the way those fill-in-the-blank people are, so they deserve to be stepped on."

5. Once Joe has justified hurting Fred, he will continue to hurt Fred on the basis of his trumped-up justifications.

6. Joe loses respect for Fred because Fred allows himself to be hurt.

This may continue until Fred is mentally collapsed and has a nervous breakdown or worse, or until Fred finally confronts Joe and says something like, "Look, damn it! I'm not taking your @#* anymore!"

If Fred feels unworthy or inferior as a person, he may allow Joe to run him right into the ground. You may know someone, someone you consider to be a good person, who puts up with another who makes her life miserable. You wonder why she takes it. Possibly she feels unworthy of having someone nice to be with. She can't accept people being nice to her. She is attracted to people who put her down.

She has been able to handle invalidation—after all, she is surviving, isn't she? But if she should happen to get some praise or affection, she doesn't know how to deal with it.

The person who invalidates is not always the SOB. A passive-aggressive victim can create a scene in which it looks like he is being invalidated. Fred could set himself up to be invalidated by being sickeningly sweet and cowering around Joe. Did you ever meet someone you had the impulse to put down? This person might have the appearance of being the sweetest person in town, yet frequently makes unconscious, little "mistakes" without taking responsibility for them. This person might be late all the time and always have a good excuse for being late, and cower and make you look like a @#* for being upset with him. He is always putting himself down. The context of his interaction is "look how disgusting I am."

You tend to have no respect for someone who has no self-respect. When you congratulate him on something, he makes little of your congratulations because he can't have good will for himself. He may be a terrific person, and yet he will draw invalidators like a magnet. He will choose to have a lousy time with somebody you consider to be an SOB rather than a good time with you. If he is with you, he may constantly try to prove to you what a miserable, helpless loser he is. He has to be "right" in thinking that he is a victim, a lowly soul. He will set it up so the world proves this to him and to others constantly.

There is an invalidator in his past . . . and now there is an invalidator inside his head. He's internalized the invalidator and turned it against himself. But look out—his misery loves company.

An invalidator sets up a context that says, "You're wrong. You're wrong." And a victim sees herself as a victim and will not own responsibility, and she works hard to prove she really is a victim so she can be "right" about it.

The victim will bend your ear constantly about the tragedies of her life. Horrible circumstances, drunken spouse, fire-destroyed house, unemployment—and someone else is always to blame. "They" did it to her again. She will explain it in such a way that she could do nothing about it. "The car drove off the highway and hit a tree." (She just happened to be sitting there drunk behind the steering wheel.) Then they took away her license, so she lost her job. And they fired her after six months of faithful service just because she couldn't come to work. She is very interested in having you agree with her so she can feel more justified in being a victim.

This person may not appreciate anything you do for her because she feels unworthy of it. You will seldom be able to please her or make her happy. Happiness is impossible for her. These people are perfect mates for invalidators. They survive on being miserable. If things go too well for them, they will create an upset in their lives.

You may find that your efforts to help such a victim never seem to work. He always seems to mess up his life again— always unconsciously. You end up feeling impotent. And until this person recognizes his victim act and begins to do something about it, there isn't much you can do. He has to intend to change. He has to stop blaming his bad luck and his weak willpower for his problems and decide to stop being a loser.

A friend of mine met a woman who seemed to be in a bad situation. She was short on her rent, and the landlord was getting ready to boot her out. She told my friend she just needed fifty dollars and the rent would be paid. She had two children, and my friend hated to see her and her children on the street so he gave her fifty dollars. The next week he saw her and her children walking down the street and he stopped to say hello. He was surprised to hear the landlord had followed through and evicted her. "But you paid the rent," he said.

"Well, you know," she started, "I was going to the landlord to give him the rent, and I passed by this dress store, and they had a dress that I had been looking at for a long time. It was on sale for only forty-five dollars. I couldn't pass it up."

A person's integrity is based on his or her intentions. If a person intends to be valuable and intends to be worthy, then there is no stopping her. She will give up proving how unworthy she is. Each person's worth is determined by that person alone. If she knows she has good intentions, then she may encounter barriers to her self-realization and make mistakes on the way, but there is no proving that she is a rotten person or a miserable loser. There is no way to make her a victim, once she has decided not to be one anymore.

Her life can be focused on developing her magnificence and not on the mistakes or barriers that temporarily get in her way. She intends to free herself, and her intention frees her.

Two Dancers: An Example

Let's compare two dancers, looking at the way each one handles a setback in his practice.

The first dancer intends to do step X. He fails. He intends to do step X. He fails. He intends to do step X. He succeeds.

This dancer has focused his attention on the magnificence of his dancing. He pays attention to what he intends to do, and he knows how to let go of the mistakes.

The second dancer wants to do step X. He fails. He complains about the slippery floor. He decides he will never get it right. He compares his dancing to that of the first dancer and feels inferior. He wants to do step X. He fails. He gets depressed. He dwells on what a rotten dancer he is. He

blames his parents for not sending him to ballet school when he was younger. He blames the world for being so unfair that he was raised in a family with no money. He wants really badly to do step X. Finally, he either gives up or does step X at last.

If he finally succeeds in doing step X, he may then compare himself to a lesser dancer who can't even do step X yet and demonstrate his incredible ego.

Meanwhile, the first dancer has gone on to do steps Y and Z.

This chapter is not about two types of persons. If what you thought you got from this chapter is the ability to run around pinning labels of "victim" or "invalidator" on real people, then you didn't get much from this chapter. This chapter is describing and identifying phenomena that may partially or wholly exist in an individual. If you use the data in this book to make someone wrong . . . then this book is about you.

Pointing out invalidation to another for the purpose of handling it is not invalidating that person (although he or she may feel invalidated). Pointing out invalidation to another for the purpose of making him or her wrong is invalidating. It's the intention behind the words and actions that makes all the difference. In handling invalidation, you can get great confidence from knowing your intentions.

Nearly everyone has some of the traits of an invalidator. The one-percenter does it consciously, consistently, for personal gain, for power, for control, and without conscience.

But everyone falls into the role of invalidator sometimes. Do you invalidate? Probably! You may do it when you feel someone has wronged you. You may do it as a defense. You may do it unconsciously. The next section of this book is addressed to the invalidator. It may help you recognize what someone is doing to you. But it also may help you recognize when you are the invalidator.

3

THE CYCLE OF INVALIDATION

Every time you meet a situation, though you think at the time it is an impossibility and you go through the tortures of the damned, once you have met it and lived through it, you find that forever after you are freer than you were before.
—ELEANOR ROOSEVELT

In this chapter I address the reader who may have decided that he or she is an invalidator and I present an examination of the cycle of invalidation. Later in the chapter I address the reader who has decided he or she is being invalidated.

To an Invalidator

So, you have decided you are an invalidator. Or else you are not quite sure you are an invalidator. Or else you don't consider yourself to be an invalidator, but you are reading this section to see what the author will have to say to "them." If you admit to being an invalidator, you have my respect and acknowledgment for your willingness to confront this part of yourself.

We all react to things. Some hurt others. Some hurt themselves. The secret behind changing it is your intention and willingness to know. That's about it. It may sound simple. Actually, it is sometimes simple and sometimes very hard. Thank you for being willing to read this. Now that you've read more than half of my book and I've described the invalidator in great detail, I want you to know that I know there is no such thing as an invalidator. That's right. There are only people and the mechanism of invalidation. It was my approach to use the term *invalidator*. If you thought you were—ta da!—an invalidator, that just shows how willing you are to put yourself down.

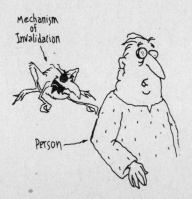

If you find yourself invalidating, work on that mechanism. Get out of that destructive role, you ol' invalidator, you!

Maybe you think this doesn't really tell you how to stop invalidating. You want to stop right now. Well, tough. Your impatience is showing. If you read this chapter and understand it, then you will have the ability to clear that up for yourself. It will take time. I forgot to mention this: another trait of an invalidator is impatience.

Why You Are an Invalidator

There aren't too many people who wake up in the morning and say to themselves, "From now on, I am going to put people down and make them feel lousy." Invalidation is learned, not inherent. There is a reason you have become an invalidator. Was there someone in your life who invalidated you? It could have been someone you loved or someone you hated. Invalidation is a mechanism that gets passed on from one to another. Who in your life was always "right"? Under whose thumb were you? Of whom were you afraid? These questions may assist you in locating a possible invalidator in your life. Who invalidated you, or who did you see invalidate others?

If you feel bad about yourself for invalidating, then chances are feeling bad about yourself will cause you to invalidate even more. Chances are good that you invalidate yourself more than anyone. You may feel like such an SOB, you may be so down on yourself, that you think someone who would love you must be even worse than you are and therefore deserving of being invalidated. After all, anyone who would hang around with such a creep as you are must be really screwed up. Right?

How Do You Stop?

So, what should you do if you catch yourself invalidating and decide you'd like to stop doing it? Well, hang on to your hat and get ready to confront some things about yourself.

Maybe at some point in your life, someone made you so wrong that you succumbed to being wrong, and you agreed that you were wrong. After that, you considered yourself to be basically wrong or basically screwed up. You may also have made the assumption that others are basically nasty, too.

You may have spent a lot of your life proving that you were not messed up because you don't want to appear bad. So you feel as if you have to be righteous about yourself. You have to be right all the time. Well, now, how did all this come about?

It happened through the mechanism of invalidation, which gets passed from one person to another and one generation to another by contagion. Again, there is really no such thing as an invalidator. There is a person, and then aside from the person is the mechanism of invalidation. A person may use this mechanism, but the mechanism is not the person. You may sometimes be attached to invalidation so closely you cannot see it. Sometimes you may feel the effect of invalidating. You may know you are doing it, you don't want to, you don't like yourself for doing it to people, and still you just keep on doing it. It can be so frustrating that you finally just give up and accept yourself as an SOB. You define yourself as "bad," and you dramatize invalidation. You constantly find yourself invalidating, just as you yourself were invalidated. You feel compelled to do it. It seems to happen automatically sometimes because you identified with the invalidator.

You think you have only two choices:

1. Be like the invalidator and *survive*.
2. Be like the invalidated and succumb.

You may come to believe that you must hurt or be hurt, control or be controlled. After all, in your past experience, the invalidator won and you lost. You *reenact*. Get it? You repeat the whole drama, but this time you try to be the winner, the SOB who can't be defeated.

You may reenact in certain situations, almost like a machine. That's not you out there; that's just your dramatization of negative experiences you had years ago. When you are reenacting, or invalidating someone automatically because it was once done to you, who really gets invalidated?

If there ever was a Satan, he wouldn't have wanted to work very hard to pollute souls. He probably would have resorted to inventing a set of nasty archetypes that would spread from one person to another by contagion. After all, if he was so evil, he wouldn't want to struggle. It would be easier to throw a couple pieces of junk into still water and watch it ripple. So he invented invalidation! And he made it contagious. We did the rest.

Maybe sometimes you are not into invalidation and sometimes you are. It may almost seem that you are two different people, one who has good intentions and is very supportive, and one who sometimes takes over, making you into an "invalidation entity." This evil entity is not you, but a role you are playing: the role of invalidator.

You probably feel a sense of unreality when you are in that role. You act very controlling, but you may feel that you are being controlled. You may appear to others to be very demanding and authoritative. But inside you feel very helpless and scared. That demanding, authoritarian, invalidating entity is your act, which you reenact over and over again.

If you are a one-percenter you know exactly what you are doing. For other invalidators, it is not that way. They invalidate because their buttons get pushed. It's hard to understand sometimes, because it's not about a motive or any particular result. It's about the *drama*. If your potential victim can rise above it and not take it personally, the drama will soon subside. Otherwise you are going to "get into it" with that other person.

What Happens to Invalidators?

Two things happen to invalidators. Some see that invalidation doesn't work in the long run. This can happen through life hints. If you get enough of these hints and are paying attention, your behavior changes. Some of the hints may be small (e.g., people avoid you, no one sits next to you at a party). Some may be as big as the "hand of reality" rising out of the situation and smacking you hard (e.g., your spouse joins the circus or runs off with a circus performer).

But, as we discussed earlier, not everyone gets the hint, and then what happens is rather sad. Instead of going through the natural cycle that others go through when they hurt people, you can't admit being wrong. You have more of a deny-and-suppress pattern that suppresses guilt and disrespects (blames) the victim. The suppressed guilt stays inside and gathers until you begin to feel depressed or you become psychosomatically ill.

THE MECHANISM OF INVALIDATION

Person A invalidates Person B, the victim.
   Person A = the invalidator
   Person B = the invalidated

Characteristics of Person A
   Feels inadequate
   Feels angry
   Feels compelled to control
   Unwilling to listen
   Unwilling to be wrong
   Unwilling to introvert (to look at own motives)

Characteristics of Person B
At First
Willing to listen

Willing to be wrong

Willing to introvert (to look at own motives)

After Association with Person A
Unexpressed anger

Feeling of being wrong

Feeling of inability to control

After Prolonged Association

Defines self as bad, wrong

To protect self, becomes:

Unwilling to listen

Unwilling to be wrong

Unwilling to introvert (to look at own motives)

Finally, to survive

Identifies with invalidator

Does what the invalidator does (has control, appears right, wins)

SO THE CYCLE BEGINS AGAIN

Person B has been transformed from the victim of Person A to the invalidator of Person C. Person B is now reenacting in the archetype of invalidator. Invalidation is contagious.

Person B = the invalidator
Person C = the invalidated

Characteristics of Person B

Feels inadequate
Feels angry (the anger finally surfaces but is directed
at an innocent bystander)
Feels compelled to control (out of fear of being
controlled again)
Unwilling to listen
Unwilling to be wrong
Unwilling to introvert (to look at own motives)

Characteristics of Person C

Willing to listen
Willing to be wrong
Willing to introvert (to look at own motives)

The demonic personality is a kind of manic state. Those of you in this state seem to have no conscience; you seem to enjoy manipulating and putting other people down. In this phase, you are carefree. You don't notice and don't care about the feelings of others. You go right on doing selfish things like drinking, playing around on your wife, or belittling others until, unexpectedly, you suddenly fall apart.

Then you enter an exaggerated state of remorse or get very sick as your relationships with everyone start to fall apart. You get sick, especially if your spouse leaves you, so the spouse feels obligated to come back and take care of you. The illness punishes you and gets the spouse back at the same time. You don't like your spouse's leaving, but you respect her more for doing it. Some of you feel you have been punished and now the slate is clean. Others may not feel the same way due to all the built-up resentment.

The rest of us must beware those of you who don't get sick and do not have remorse. This is bad news. Your cycle is different. You don't really care about anyone but yourself. You are extremely selfish. You are conscious of your invalidating and probably even work at perfecting it. You are the Hitler, the one-percenter. (Previously in this chapter we talked about the twenty-percenters. The twenty-percenters have enough conscience left to feel remorse at least.)

The one-percenters destroy people. The people around you are afraid of you but in your control. You are not a total devil; no one is. Most of the time you lead what looks like a normal life. It's just that you are so selfish and possessive. And, every once in a while, you do something that will make a lasting scar on someone close to you. By the time you are done living your lifetime, the world is worse for your having been here.

You are selfish. You have no conscience. You are controlling of others and manipulative. You have no sympathy and no mercy. You could even drive someone crazy or lead someone to commit suicide. People wonder how you get away with it. People wonder why you live that way. People wonder what will ever happen to you. I think I can tell you that. I've watched a person like this lead her life.

I watched helplessly while an invalidator ruthlessly invalidated his wife to suicide. It was a nonstop, merciless deed. He showed no conscience even though he had been with her for forty years. Of course, she was into a victim act and eventually made herself so weak she couldn't stand up to him anymore. She died on the day she committed suicide. He had been dead long before that.

The tools of invalidation are available for you to use right now. You or anyone can pick them up, practice them, and perfect them with repetition. But if you think invalidating people is a good way of controlling others, think twice.

Let's suppose you made use of a demonic archetype in which you were selfish and manipulative. Eventually you would really hurt someone, and then a natural remorse would tap you on the shoulder to remind you of your misdeeds. You might drop the selfish behavior and atone, get depressed, or get sick.

You use these mechanisms on a "buy now, pay later" plan. Sure, you can run around feeling carefree, not caring about others, for a while. But sooner or later you are going to end up alone and lonely. People eventually catch on, no matter how gregarious and fun-loving you are. Once people realize that you are completely taken up with yourself, they get turned off. Besides, there seems to be a natural law that eventually leads to the destruction of a person like you. After all, how can you remain a human being and constantly destroy your own foundations as a human being (empathy, caring, and conscience)?

If you repress remorse, you repress all feelings to that same degree. You also give up part of your ability to gauge how other people feel. So each time you repress real remorse, you die a little. You cannot lose touch with your own conscience without losing touch with others, because

your conscience is the bridge that connects you to others. Empathy and conscience go hand in hand.

The worst thing that can happen is that you become so selfish that you mess up all of your relationships. You lose contact so badly that you can't relate to other people at all. You lose your own feelings so that you can no longer experience love, beauty, friendship, or any of the meaningful experiences in life. You have to resort to booze, drugs, or degraded sex to feel anything at all. It's only the fleeting sensations, the "wow" moments, that are fun. You avoid anything meaningful.

You don't have to take my word for all this. I am sure you have met other invalidators who are so far gone into themselves that they have lost their ability to relate to people. They constantly invalidate others. They are also prone to moodiness or depression because nobody can stay in that totally selfish pattern forever.

If you think you can ever be happy living that way, think again. Watch for invalidation so you can handle it. Know exactly what it is. Know it and see it and sidestep it. Make invalidation lose its effect.

When someone tells you of something you did wrong, take a look at her intention in telling you that. Even if what she says is absolutely true, even if you did exactly what she is saying you did, look at her intention. Is she invalidating you, or is she trying to wise you up for your own sake?

And look at your own intentions. When you criticize someone or point out a mistake or a misdeed, are you doing it for that person's own good or to hurt?

When you are angry, do you get angry at innocent bystanders? Do you have to get mad at someone? Can you get angry freely at inanimate objects, or just get angry, period? If you need a whipping boy, clean up your act. Anger should be expressed appropriately, *not* at an innocent person. The smaller picture is the need to vent. The bigger picture is the friendship or marriage that you may be causing harm.

When you detect an invalidator, whether it's someone near you or you yourself, show a little compassion. This poor unfortunate soul is either in hell or on his way. And what is more, never label anyone an invalidator. People are people. What people do is what people do. Attacking a person instead of attacking what that person is doing just doesn't work in the long run. You're just letting invalidation breed invalidation.

To the Invalidated Who Doesn't Invalidate

Well, now, you are the "victim" of invalidation, but you don't invalidate. Ah, yes. You are not like those others. You never put anyone down. You never get angry. You were connected to an invalidator at one time, and you see it all now. So, now you're reading about them with a big halo glimmering about two inches above your head.

You don't know how to get angry without hurting people, so you hold it all inside. You were made to feel so wrong at one point that you made a forced decision that you were completely OK. That's where you got your halo.

Along with that decision, you developed an unwillingness to be wrong. But you made out better than some people; you didn't lose your willingness to listen.

Now you do the flip side of the work of an invalidator. You listen to people. You make people right. You never get angry. You've been invalidated by someone, and you certainly don't want to hurt people the way that person did. So you become dishonest with your true feelings. You fool people to build their egos.

So, now you believe you are perfectly OK. You are afraid to look at anything that doesn't agree with that premise. Being something of a pompous ass by now, you won't look at ways you could change, because that would be admitting there is something wrong with you. To you, this idea is very frightening. Instead of seeing a change in your thinking as self-improvement, you feel ashamed of it, as a sign that something is wrong with you. However, the paradox is that to be perfect, you have to be willing to look at your imperfections. It is especially difficult for someone who has been made to feel wrong to be willing to appear wrong. Your willingness to be wrong has been abused. You may now have a big scar there, and you may feel completely vulnerable.

If you have made a defensive decision that you are perfectly OK, you might desperately try to hold on to this state. You might become terribly opposed to change. You were once in a situation where deciding you were OK meant your ego survival. So you will go to great lengths to maintain this belief. If you are approached with a mistake you are making, or if someone sees you are in trouble and tries to help, you may react with fear. If you find yourself changing your opinions or your point of view, you may become terrified and feel you are finally succumbing as you almost did to the invalidator long ago. You may quickly escape from any change and fall back on your old beliefs. You are willing to look at new ideas only if they do not threaten your basic determination that you are OK right now, just as you are, and you always have been perfectly OK. You may be perceived by others as a weird person, because your mind becomes a mishmash of modern ideas and antiquated attitudes. You may develop a lot of funny quirks in your personality, because nothing can be allowed to shake the foundations of the basic structure you are holding on to.

A healthy person realizes that he is OK, and he can accept other people's opinions and judgments. He is willing to see that sometimes someone else can be right and he can be wrong, and that helps keep his feelings in balance. But if a person has been forced to define himself as perfectly OK in order to defend himself against someone who wanted to invalidate him, he may not be able to accept opinions other than his own. It was the judgments of another person that pushed him to this defensive position in the first place, so now he feels he can never be wrong, especially if his mistake is pointed out by another person.

A likable personality—one that never gets angry and always builds egos—is the flip side of the invalidator personality. But this character type has its problems, too. The invalidator sprays anger all over, and this causes problems for her victims and for herself. But the victim who cannot and will not express any anger at all represses his anger and probably has to repress most of his other feelings along with it. Both feel righteous. Both feel inadequate. The only way out of this trap is to be able to listen, express anger constructively, be wrong, and change when the situation requires it. And if everyone could live that way, there would be no invalidators!

4

WHAT DO WE DO ABOUT IT?

Only the weak are cruel. Gentleness can only be
expected from the strong.
—Leo Buscaglia

In this chapter I will propose several aspects of handling invalidation, from coping with an invalidator boss or spouse; to general reasoning approaches; to specific approaches for confronting invalidators such as getting them alone and mirroring their projection; to what to tell children about a bully.

Invalidator Boss

What do you do if your boss invalidates constantly? Let's be practical about this.

You could decide he is just an SOB. You could set out to get him for all the misery you've endured. This wouldn't say much for your integrity, and you'd have to live with yourself, knowing that your intentions were vengeful. It would also justify your boss's outlook on life. Your boss might expect this of people. Besides, it wouldn't work.

You could tell him off. This would allow you to release your pent-up emotion, but it wouldn't work. He might invalidate you more than ever, and you might not keep your job, let alone get a raise.

You probably won't be able to reason with your boss while he is in his demon personality. It's better to wait until he is himself. If the demon is all there is to your boss, then I suggest you start looking for a new job right now. He may be too far gone to help or to deal with at all.

One thing you know: if he is invalidating you, he must have learned it from somebody, possibly a domineering mother or a controlling father. It may not have been either of his parents, but maybe his boss. Maybe he thinks that's

the way a boss is supposed to act. It has happened that, if the president of the company is a habitual invalidator, everyone down the line takes on that behavior. After all, it is contagious.

More than anything else, an invalidator has to be right. Never, never say "You're wrong" to an invalidator; this is a cardinal rule. If you contradict, point out, demonstrate, or in any way show an invalidator to be wrong, sooner or later he will get you. Sooner or later you will pay. Invalidators are extremely revengeful. To an invalidator, being wrong is the most horrible thing that can happen to him, and he will not thank the person who puts him in that position. The best thing to do is acknowledge an invalidator; this does not mean to agree.

Here's an example. An invalidator shares his opinion with you about the other employees. She says, "You know, those people out there are all for themselves. Nobody cares about this department." The worst thing you can say is, "No, you're wrong. Those people are dedicated and concerned people." The best thing you can do is to acknowledge what she says and try to see if there is some reason she said it. You might say, "You think so?" in such a vague way as to acknowledge what she said and allow her to talk more about it. There may be something specific that makes her think that way. Perhaps she just walked by someone who took an extra two minutes at break time. Later, when she isn't being critical and doesn't suspect that you are trying to prove her wrong, you can point out some unselfish things the employees have done.

One thing that invalidators respond to best is affinity. If you like him, he may even allow you to prove him wrong once in a while. That goes for almost anyone, of course. If you like someone and show that person a great deal of affinity, you can say practically anything to him. Be sure you always do it in private. An invalidator takes "being wrong" in front of a group as a terrible humiliation.

If you show that you like your boss, you will gain benefits beyond reason. Invalidators are excellent at logic, so they don't put much stock in it. But affinity is something they lack, and they can use a lot of it. After all, someone in this person's past probably chewed him up with logic and pushed him away at the same time.

Research shows that one of the most significant causes of hostility (and bullying) is a lack of nurturing. Lack of nurturing? Yes. What does that mean? That means that what the kid down the block who bullies your kids needs is nurturing. That's what is going to work. It's the very thing you don't want to give, but it's the thing that works the best. That kid is going to grow up and become someone's boss or spouse. What will he still need? Right, nurturing.

I was researching all this when my sister called me. She was student teaching and had a kid in her class who was driving her crazy. She was concerned that she wouldn't get a good evaluation because the kid was such a distraction. He berated the other kids and her under his breath. He was really disrespectful and was an overall pain. She asked me what to do because I am the family shrink, and I told her I would tell her but she had to promise to do it.

She said, "Tell me first."

I said, "No. Promise first."

She was desperate, so she promised. I said, "You have to nurture this kid."

"What?" she yelled. "I don't want to nurture him. I want to kick him in the pants. I am not even sure I like this kid."

I replied, "Well, then, you have to *make* yourself like him."

"OK," she said, relenting. "How do I do this?"

I told her I wasn't sure, but if it were me, I would greet the kid every day. I would try to make physical contact (appropriately, of course), and I would say, "How are you doing today, Johnny?" Then when I was lecturing, I would walk by him and touch him, just to let him know that I knew he was there.

A few days passed and I called her up and asked her how it was going. She said, "It's going too well." She continued. "He is my little sidekick now. I can't get rid of him. He tells the other kids to shut up while I am talking."

So, it seemed to work well. Now back to the boss.

It helps if you can find a genuine reason to look up to your boss. Invalidators are usually me-me-me people. Their self-esteem is actually low, but they hide this well by displaying overinflated egos. An invalidator may think of himself as the only important person around, but he may feel inferior to others. He uses his self-inflation to try to make up for the inferiority. It's a confusing paradox—but ignore it at your peril.

With this knowledge, you can realize that the apparently strong, confident, ruthless boss might actually feel inside like a scared little kid. He may be someone to be pitied, not someone to be feared.

It's ironic, but the best way to make an invalidator lose his grip is to invalidate him. A person who is trying to hurt another will use the methods that he would find hurtful. If you want to hurt an invalidator, all you need to do is watch what he does or says to others. If you use his own methods against him, he will cave in sooner than anyone. It's so obvious it's almost funny. I'm not suggesting that you take advantage of this knowledge. Just know that whatever your boss is doing was done to him. You could "win" if you utilize this knowledge.

If you choose this method, you should realize that you may be putting your job on the line. This may actually be the most positive career step you can make, though it can be a hard one. You may want to line up another job before you try it. Invalidating your boss may give you a feeling of satisfaction as you stand in the unemployment line.

If your boss embarrasses you in front of a group and you want to get him back, embarrass him in front of a group. But be careful. He has probably been embarrassing people in groups for years and is probably much better at it than you are. But you'll have the benefit of surprise, so his endurance won't be as good.

Invalidator Spouse

It is typical for one partner in a marriage to be dominant. Someone has to have the final say, or marriages wouldn't work. It is probably best if the responsibilities are divided up so that each gets to have the final say about half the time. That way, each one is the boss sometimes. That makes for a happy relationship.

But how many marriages do you know of that are happy? The spousal relationship generally has more invalidation in it than any other. It is a worldwide disease. It seems as if the usual pattern is to get married, eventually do irreversible harm to the relationship, and end up divorced or having regret about getting married.

One of the problems of our society is that we can't seem to rehabilitate a marriage once it has gone bad. We wait until things are intolerable before we seek help. Then we don't really want help; we want out. It is similar to the situation of people who did drugs in the sixties. Some caused themselves permanent damage. They now say, "If only I had known back then."

Just because someone seems to be controlling the family doesn't mean he is necessarily an invalidator. His spouse could simply be irresponsible; someone has to manage things.

There are lots of "nice" ways to invalidate, too, like the silent treatment, when a spouse doesn't acknowledge what her husband said, or when a spouse tells his legitimately irate wife that she looks cute when she's angry.

A person using invalidation could be perfectly unconscious of doing so. The victim could also be unconscious of
it. Whether the invalidator and victim (or two invalidators!)
are conscious or unconscious of their patterns, two people
who initially love each other can get caught up in this sce-
nario, and it degrades the whole family over time. The person doing most of the invalidating does not become aware
of it until it is too late, when the love has died and the damage is irreparable.

Have you ever met someone who was surprised when her
spouse left? Things were so wonderful, and then *bang* . . .
he runs off with a circus performer! It could have been
unconscious invalidation at work.

Even if the invalidator is made aware, he may not be
made properly aware. He may just suppress his invalidating
tendencies instead of correcting them. He may hold back
his feelings instead of learning how to let them out constructively. Sooner or later, the old behavior unleashes itself,
and he loses relationship after relationship.

Many times, the invalidator is not motivated to change,
because she is the "winner." She has these powerful mechanisms backing her up, so she doesn't suffer in the short
run. Often, however, she damages the marriage perma-
nently before she is aware of it.

While it is true that some people are irreversible invalidators, there aren't that many of them. It's worth making
the effort to break the negative pattern of invalidation. If

the invalidator finds that invalidation no longer works, he might be motivated to change. If you are being invalidated by your spouse, it's *your* problem. Once you no longer allow the invalidator to control you, he will finally have to deal with himself; his problems remain his.

Try the following:

1. Identify the problem for the invalidator.
2. Set limits for behavior of the invalidator—what is and is not acceptable to you.
3. Set a time limit for change.
4. Pay attention to what the invalidator does rather than what he or she says.

If invalidation is a way of life for your spouse, you may have no alternative but to separate. However, I have found that in many cases, the marriage is fixable. Also, be sure that you are not leaving just to invalidate your spouse!

Handling Invalidation

If we wanted to, we could fit all the ways of handling things into two categories:

1. **Reason.** For example, a parent says to her child, "Don't go out into the street, dear, because you may get hit by a car."

2. **Cause-effect.** For example, a parent says to his child, "You went out into the street *again*!" and gives the child a little smack on the butt.

People who have great reasoning capabilities sometimes nevertheless have a great deal of trouble understanding cause-effect solutions. Their world is very logical, and they may have had great success solving situations using logic. They tend to believe that almost anything can be handled with reason and logic. They tend to be philosophical about life and try to be very fair about everything. And perhaps they are a little afraid of things that are irrational or beyond comprehension. (These are the people who were incapable of believing that Hitler was herding Jews into gas furnaces by the millions.) These people are easy to invalidate because they naively believe in the good intent of everyone. They think it is a joke or slip of the tongue if someone cuts into them.

Then there are people who do not put much stock in logic, reason, or philosophy. These people have been manipulated by it, lied to by it, and deceived by it. They have learned to pay more attention to what people do rather than to what they say. These are the ones who fire you because you called in sick too often . . . no matter what the reason. They may appear to be listening to you, but actually they will be looking at your expressions and actions, trying to size you up by your appearance rather than your thought processes.

Mr. Reason and Mr. Cause-Effect do not have a very good understanding of one another when they are in their purest form, because they are at opposite ends of a continuum:

Reason   Cause-Effect

←——————————————————————————————→

Thank goodness most of us are somewhere in between. There is no right or wrong about it. Perhaps when confronting invalidation a balanced approach would be most effective. Mr. Cause-Effect Boss does not want to hear about any problems with making a deadline. He will see any reasons not to do so as "excuses" or "rationalizing." To him, it's simple. You either make it or you don't. On the good side, he can't be given any bull. On the dark side, he is not going to listen to reason.

Mr. Reason Boss will listen to his employees. He will understand why a deadline cannot be met. On the dark side, people may be able to pull the wool over his eyes. He may end up accepting rationalizations and excuses, to the demise of the company.

Both of these extremes have blind spots in their narrow vision. A balanced boss would be cause-effect when she had to be. She may threaten an employee with the loss of his job if the employee is not performing, even if he is clever enough to make rational-sounding excuses. A balanced boss would listen to a valuable employee who was going through a rough time and make exceptions in a deadline if she could.

There is no set of rules to handle invalidation that work every time, but let's take a look at a sequence that may meet with some success.

First try **reason**. Handle the invalidator with the following approaches:

- Humor
- Respect
- Affinity and personableness
- Professionalism
- Acknowledgment
- Diplomacy
- Patience
- Discretion
- Firmness
- Words that tell how you feel

Don't do any of the following:

- Generalize
- Label
- Judge
- Blame
- Make him or her wrong
- Be righteous
- Make it personal

- Insinuate
- Act out your angry feelings
- Make him or her feel guilty

If reasoning doesn't work, try **cause-effect**:

- Hurt the invalidator when he or she invalidates.
- Invalidate him or her. (Show the invalidator how it feels.)
- Do something outrageous. (Talk loudly. Act crazy. Squirt the invalidator with a water gun. Laugh shrilly as if the invalidator just told you a joke. Wink at the invalidator. Make raspberry noises.)
- Insult the invalidator.
- Squeeze his or her cheek.
- Raise your eyebrows.
- Stare unwaveringly.
- Disconnect/quit/leave.

The cause-effect reactions you give to invalidators make them uncomfortable whenever they invalidate. I had a psychology professor whom a bunch of us tried to manipulate using behavioral techniques. He used to pace back and forth across the room, and it was annoying to us. So every time he walked over to the right, we would yawn or act bored. When he walked to the left, we would act attentive. By the end of the semester, he was sitting on a stool to the far left of the room without ever knowing our little plot!

If your invalidator actually likes any of the above cause-effect reactions and enters into a game with you, stop doing what you are doing and move on to another reaction in your cause-effect arsenal. Get the idea?

Drug dealers keep selling drugs because they go to court and nothing happens. If the drug dealer is a cause-effect person, he will say the right things or get the right lawyer and get out on probation. In his mind, nothing happened! In some cases, one good punch in the nose would give the dealer enough of a "reality adjustment" that he would say to himself, "Ouch! That hurt! No more selling drugs for me!" Research shows that swift adjudication significantly lowers the rate of recidivism (coming back to jail). Likewise, cause-effect invalidators need to see or feel a result of their actions. The more immediate the result, the better.

Again, I must remind you that if you know all the approaches, you can find a way to deal with invalidation that fits your personality and your ethics. No book can cover every situation. You won't be a pro handler of invalidation from reading this book, just as you won't be a pro baseball player from reading a guidebook to baseball. All you get are the rules.

That said, because people ask me for some specific things that they can try, I am going to give you some approaches that seem to work most of the time and some examples of what I have seen others do to confront invalidation. Please remember, however, to do it your way.

Confronting

What a great approach confronting is! You just look at the person who invalidated you in such a way that you show you know exactly what she is doing. A long pause or a knowing smile, resting your chin in your hand or leaning forward slightly, can let her know she had better not mess with you.

Here is an example. A father-in-law has been asking (interrogating) his son-in-law about his job all evening at dinner, looking for buttons to push. Finally, the father-in-law gets red in the face, turns on fire eyes and booming voice and says, "What kind of a job is that for a man to have?" The son-in-law says nothing but keeps looking at the father-in-law calmly. The father-in-law raises his voice, increases the red color, and opens his eyes wider while ranting and raving. The son-in-law still just looks at him calmly. Finally the father-in-law looks away, rants and raves to the other people at the table, lowers his voice, gets up from the table, and leaves.

The son-in-law did not "get into it." He did not cower. He did not agree or give in. He maintained contact with the father-in-law. The father-in-law felt uncomfortable enough to leave and won't be inclined to attack him again.

Repeat That, Please

Asking the person to repeat the invalidation will many times cause her to water it down, especially if it was an insinuation or something that she was trying to sneak by you. If she is brave enough to repeat it again arrogantly, you can say, "Oh. That's what I thought you said." Usually, however, the coward will not repeat it the way she said it the first time.

Tell the Whole Truth

A lot of invalidations are double messages riddled with insinuations, voice inflections, tone, and other clues besides the actual words. All you need to do is to size up everything and tell the simple truth.

Here's one example. A woman attends a professional meeting with her peer group, which is made up mostly of men. Frank says, "Susan, take the minutes of the meeting, would you, dear?" Caught off guard, Susan says, "I wasn't prepared to take the minutes." Frank says beratingly, "Come on, Susan! You came to this meeting unprepared!?"

Susan's reply: "Frank, you are talking as if it is my job to take the minutes of this meeting. I suggest you ask one of us to take the minutes before the meeting starts instead of waiting till the last minute and having to make these arrangements after the meeting starts."

Susan did not get defensive. She did not accuse Frank of asking her to take the minutes just because she was a woman. She did not let him push her buttons (that is, introvert her). She merely stated things that were factual and thereby made Frank's attitude obvious.

Here's a second example. At work Al is presenting the proposal for a project he is working on. Bill is sitting at the meeting looking more and more irritated. Bill's face is red. He is breathing loudly and exasperatedly. No one understands what Al is saying because they are caught up in wondering what is bothering Bill. Finally Al addresses Bill: "Bill, is there something you want to say?"

Bill stands up with the veins popping out of his temples and says, "I sure do want to say something! You don't know what the hell you are talking about. Why, I've never seen . . ."

Al nails him with the truth. Al has to raise his voice to get above Bill's: "Bill, you came in here and were acting irritated even before I started my presentation. I don't see how you could make a judgment based only on what I have said so far. I want you to show me the respect to let me finish my presentation."

"Yeah?!" says Bill. "Well, this presentation is a waste of my time."

Al's reply is the truth: "Bill, you are embarrassing me in front of all these people. I'd like them to make up their own minds about what I am going to say. You don't have to stay at the meeting. I can talk to you later if you like."

With that, Bill stomps out of the meeting saying, "I'm not interested in what you have to say."

Al says to the group, "Why don't we take a five-minute stretch break."

The break allows everyone to talk the scene out instead of think about it during Al's presentation.

You can always tell the truth by looking at your feelings:

- "I feel embarrassed."
- "I feel angry that you said it that way."
- "I feel put on the spot."

No one can argue with the way you feel, because right or wrong it is the way you feel.

Get Him or Her Alone

A person who embarrasses you in front of a group uses the group for her power. If you get her alone, you may find that she squirms in her seat and becomes apologetic. She learns to have respect for you because she knows you will confront her instead of hiding behind a group. Reason with her first. If she embarrasses you again, threaten to do the same to her. "How would you like it if I embarrassed you in front of everyone? Do it to me again, and I will surprise you."

The surprise is you simply tell the truth. "Jane, there you go again trying to embarrass me in front of everyone. Can't you think of a more professional way to handle yourself?"

Mirror the Projection

When someone accuses you of something you didn't do, check to see if he has done it. When someone threatens you with something, threaten him back with the very same thing. Chances are he is threatening you with what he is most afraid of. When someone accuses you of not liking him or of being prejudiced, guess who doesn't like whom? Guess who is prejudiced? When someone tells you that you must choose A or B, tell him you are not going to choose, and he can choose what to do about it.

Here's one example. Dave says, "Look, it's either me or your career." Mary responds, "I'm not choosing."

Here's a second example. Fred says, "I don't think you like me." You say, "Do you like me, Fred?"

Here's a third example. Martha says, "I think you have been taking money from the business for yourself." You say, "Have you taken any money that you haven't told me about?"

What to Tell Children About Invalidators

Children can best perceive invalidators as bullies. If you think about it, that's what they really are. These bullies grow up and become your boss, your spouse, your professor in college, or your neighbor. Our society sees bullying as a natural thing. Most of us have had to deal with bullies and we consider it a rite of passage. But it isn't. It is abuse that is allowed to go on in our society because we do not take the steps necessary to solve it as a systemic problem. If bullies were dealt with effectively as children, there would be a lot less invalidation in the world.

A child who witnesses invalidation to a third party can be profoundly affected by it. It has been shown from the Vietnam War that people who witness someone getting shot have Posttraumatic Stress Disorder, right along with the ones who actually took the bullets. If a child sees a classmate being bullied, he realizes it may just as easily happen to him. Some of our children have Posttraumatic Stress Disorder from watching the hijacked planes that crashed into the World Trade Center towers on September 11, 2001. We have to be very careful how we approach invalidation because it has such a profound effect on children. Kathy Noll's book, *Taking the Bully by the Horns*, speaks to this subject in detail using children's terms based upon the principles in this book.

Usually, people are mean for one of these reasons:

1. They didn't get nurturing.
2. They want to get their way.
3. Someone was nasty to them.
4. They don't feel good about themselves.
5. They have a chemical imbalance.

Sometimes someone who doesn't feel good about himself will think you are better than he is, so he tries to make you look small. Then he can feel better. The best thing to do is to show that person that you care about him and that he is OK. If you are mean to him, you'll just be "proving" to him that he is as bad as he thinks he is. But if you point out what you like about him, he may feel better—you have made him realize he has some good qualities. If he realizes he is OK too, he won't have to be nasty.

Sometimes it's hard to find something good about someone. So then you might say that person has nice eyes or is strong. Sometimes you don't have to say anything. A pat on the back and a smile will help. It doesn't always work. Some people can be so mean that it is best to just stay away from them.

When a person is mean to you, you must remember that *you are OK*. Maybe she didn't like something you did, but you are OK. If she is mean for no reason, maybe she is just in a bad mood or she has a miserable life. Don't feel bad about yourself. Try to look at her and see why she is mean. You may say, "I'm sorry you are upset. Can I do something for you?" Sometimes if you give someone a hug, that's all it takes.

But you must be careful that a person does not take advantage of you. Don't be afraid to say "No" in a friendly way. Smile, but don't give in. You don't have to do whatever he asks. If you don't think it is right, tell him, "I can't do that."

Coping with Invalidation

Realize the "invalidator" is a personality—not a person.

Invalidators usually look big but feel small. Paradoxically, they have low self-esteem but large egos.

Invalidators invalidate when they feel inferior or out of control. The one-percenters invalidate whenever they feel it will give them control and power.

No matter how manipulative in appearance, the twenty-percenter invalidators are usually unconscious, or only semi-conscious, of what they are doing.

It is very difficult, if not impossible, to deal with an invalidator while you are in a state of introversion. First extrovert—step back and take a look at the situation. Next, try to see (not figure out) what is going on. Your biggest cues are intention and feelings. Is it the invalidator's intention to hurt you or help you? Is this communication distorted? If the intention is not good and the feelings are not good, invalidation is probably taking place in one of its many forms.

Do not take it personally. Do not let your buttons get pushed. Maintain a larger view. Do not lose your situational awareness.

Invalidation is contagious. If you have been invalidated, you are more likely to slip into doing it yourself. If someone is invalidating you, he or she has probably been invalidated in the past. At first, you might slip easily in and out of the invalidator personality. But the more you use this mechanism, the more you depend on it. Finally, you seem to become the role—the invalidator. But remember, there is no such animal. There are only people and the things that people do. Anyone can become an invalidator, and anyone can stop being one.

Invalidation works in the short run, not in the long run. With it, you can win a lot of battles but lose the war.

5

TO INVALIDATION: THE MECHANISM

When good is hungry it seeks food even in dark caves.
—KAHLIL GIBRAN

My research on invalidation was prompted by experiences I personally had with the mechanism. I watched helplessly while I saw someone I cared about being invalidated literally to death. At first, I blamed the "invalidator," but then I realized that he, too, was a victim of invalidation. I wrote the following statement about the process when I was overwhelmed; it was a rather intense moment in my life. But it contains my intentions. It's a statement to invalidation itself.

To Invalidation

You are this tremendous burden that impinges on me, whether I like it or not. You take no responsibility but create more and more unwanted responsibility for me. You come from the bowels of the physical universe. You are destructive. You are evil. You kill people. You degrade people. You create egomaniacs from your evil power. You enable people to suppress via your control mechanisms. You are sneaky. You have no conscience. You abuse the cherished things in life and spoil them. You create more evil with evil. You create sickness, and you are sickness. You are one of the sinister archetypes. You re-create yourself.

People have used destructive forces to destroy you. They have killed people but not you. You have been used against yourself: invalidators have been invalidated. This has perpetuated you with the illusion that you were defeated. In crusades, the victors have to use evil to conquer, and in so doing, the victors become evil themselves. You are paradoxical. You are subtle in your righteousness. You are a quirk.

But you shall be conquered. You shall be exposed to the world. And in your nakedness you shall be helpless. You shall carry no force. You shall be anticipated. I will persist. I am not merely a Don Quixote. I know how you work. I know your weaknesses. I am not being destructive. I will not persist against you. My approach will be to extract the being from the mechanism. You as a mechanism cannot

operate except subtly, and I shall remove the subtlety and make you known. The being will see you, thereby separating himself from what you are. He will be who he is, and you will be just a mechanism. And the paradox is that no one will destroy you. They will just choose not to nourish you, and you will die.

I will do all this not out of ego, not for credit. I do it out of love for my self—my self as humanity. I do it out of choice. And I have chosen to be completely responsible for you.

I attempt to unmask you, not for the evil purpose of trying to destroy evil, but to free myself and others from this paradox. I can see, as a prophecy, that evil will diminish as a result.

I will carry my distaste for you. I will enjoy seeing you disappear. Your elimination will give me sustenance. And my purpose will be love, and not destruction. So this is the beginning of your end. When this secret is exposed, it will no longer be effective.

If you have read this far, I know you are a person who wants to improve yourself and improve the way people live around you and with you. I wanted to share "To Invalidation" with you so that together we can work a miracle for generations to come. Invalidation can be terrible for an individual, but the problem really stems from an "us" problem. I want all my great-great-grandchildren and yours to live in happiness and harmony. If we don't do something about invalidation, who will? And if we don't do it now, then when? I think it has to be us and it has to be now.

Bibliography

Berne, Eric. *Games People Play*. New York: Ballantine, 1978.

Berry, Carmen Renee. *When Helping You Is Hurting Me*. New York: Harper & Row, 1988.

Bramson, Robert. *Coping with Difficult People*. New York: Anchor Press/Doubleday, 1981.

Carter, James. *Self-Analysis: The Book About Life*. Oreland, PA: Crusader Press, 1983.

Dean, Melanie A. *Borderline Personality Disorder*. Salt Lake City: Compact Clinicals, 2001.

Drossman, Douglas A., M.D. "The Relationship Between IBS and Abuse." Internet article (iffd.org), February 2000.

English, O. Spurgeon, M.D., and Pearson, Gerald H. J., M.D. *Emotional Problems of Living*. New York: Norton, 1963.

Gibran, Kahlil. *The Prophet*. New York: Knopf, 1923.

Griffin, George. "The Case of the Costly Neurotic." Paper, March 1983.

Hare, Robert D. *Without Conscience*. New York: The Guilford Press, 1993.

Hubbard, L. Ron. *Self-Analysis*. Los Angeles: The American Saint Hill Organization, 1950.

Jung, C. G. *Man and His Symbols*. New York: Doubleday and Co., 1964.

Kiersey, David. *Please Understand Me II*. Del Mar, CA: Prometheus Nemesis Book, 1998.

Lombardo, Michael M., and Morgan, W. McCall, Jr. *Coping with an Intolerable Boss*. North Carolina: Center for Creative Leadership, 1984.

Lewis, C. S. *The Screwtape Letters*. New York: Macmillan Publishing Co., Inc., 1961.

Mondimore, Francis Mark. *Bipolar Disorder*. Baltimore: The Johns Hopkins University Press, 1999.

Noll, Kathy, with Carter, Jay. *Taking the Bully by the Horns*. Wyomissing, PA: Unicorn Press, 2001.

O'Connell, David F. *Dual Disorders*. Binghamton, NY: The Haworth Press, 1998.

Payne, Robert. *The Life and Death of Adolf Hitler*. New York: Praeger Publishers, 1973.

Prather, Hugh. *Notes on Love and Courage*. New York: Doubleday, 1977.

Sheridan, John H. "Executives at the Breaking Point." Paper, Cleveland: 1979.

Shorr, Melissa. "Belittling, Shaming Child Causes Lasting Damage." Internet article (vachss.com), April 2002.

Tannen, Deborah. *You Just Don't Understand*. New York: Ballantine, 1990.

Although I may not be able to answer all correspondence, I am interested in knowing how this book has affected your life. You may write me at the following address:

P.O. Box 6048

Wyomissing, PA 19610

Or

JayCarter.net

Or

JayCarter115@cs.com

You may also use this address to contact me regarding speaking engagements on these and other topics:

- Anger management (for corporations)
- Communication—still the number-one secret to success
- Bullies (in schools)
- Addiction (for mental health professionals and corporations)
- Dealing with difficult personalities (for corporations)
- Bipolarity (for mental health professionals and rehabilitators)
- Using the prefrontal lobe (for corporate executives or in dealing with ADD and ADHD)